D0150156

CLOSURE
and the Law of Relationship

Endings as New Beginnings

LISSA COFFEY

foreword by **Arielle Ford**

CLOSURE and the Law of Relationship:
Endings as New Beginnings

Copyright © 2010 by Lissa Coffey
Foreword © 2010 by Arielle Ford

Published by
Bamboo Entertainment, Inc.
4607 Lakeview Canyon Road Suite 181
Westlake Village, CA 91361

ISBN: 1-4392-5953-4
ISBN-13: 9781439259535

Endorsement Quotes

"Eastern philosophy teaches us that change is inevitable, and yet suffering is not. In her insightful new book, *Closure*, Lissa Coffey shows us how to learn and grow as we move through the evolution of our relationships. Highly recommended."

—Deepak Chopra
Author of *The Ultimate Happiness Prescription*

"*Closure* is the essential guide for anyone who is looking to increase their sense of peace, joy and fulfillment. Follow Lissa's wisdom and experience a total sense of enlightenment."

—Peggy McColl
New York Times Best-Selling
Author of *Your Destiny Switch*

"What is, is; your relationship is over. Now Lissa guides you through the difficult process of accepting the things you cannot change, minimizing the pain, and moving on. You'll feel better, and you'll grow as you learn. I will be giving this book to many of my hypnotherapy clients."

—Dick Sutphen
Author of *Soul Agreements*

"I loved it! As so often is the case, books that are supposed to lead us back to ourselves can be dense and complicated. Lissa's book allows the reader to understand the insight and wisdom it takes to come back to the joy. Her words reflect how much she truly cares about the healing of humanity. Brava!"

—Catherine Hickland
Actress, Author of *The 30-Day Heartbreak Cure*

"Who among us hasn't been devastated by the loss of a relationship—whether through separation, divorce, or death? Most of the time, we can't see beyond the present moment and mistakenly believe that life could never be as good without that other person in our daily lives. By the end of the journey through Lissa Coffey's book, *Closure*, we come to realize that we will be better for having loved, and life will be even sweeter when we start to live it again!"

—Shaun Robinson
TV Host, Author of *Exactly As I Am*

"There can be no doubt that Lissa Coffey knows from whence she speaks when it comes to relationships. She understands that every relationship, regardless of how good or bad it is, shall have an ending as surely as it had a beginning. Lissa shows us how to open the portal of closure and gently guides us through the opening. The result is nothing less than the peace that passes all understanding. Lissa demonstrates how closure allows us to step into the present moment where new life awaits us with open arms. That is the blessing to be found in this book."

—Dennis Merritt Jones
Author of *The Art of Being:*
101 Ways to Practice Purpose In Your Life

"Lissa is so right about her perspective to relationships. Each person with whom we bond has come into our life for a purpose. They are either a teacher to us or we are a teacher to them. When we focus on the lessons that person's interactions have taught us, then the transition of the relationship, including the ending of it, has great insight for us. All relationships are temporary, so when we embrace that closure as a transition it is easier to move through."

—Dating Goddess
Author of the *Adventures in*
Delicious Dating After 40 series

To Greg, who has always been with me,
and always will be.

To Freddy and Brian, who came through me,
and to me, to teach me so much.

To Autumn, who has me learning
and growing exponentially.

To Ryan, Ellen, and Anika, who show me that
the heart connection knows no time or space.

Table of Contents

Part 3: Reconnection

Foreword

In a lyric from his famous song, "Beautiful Boy," John Lennon assures us that "life is what happens while you're busy making other plans." Life's unexpected detours are sometimes interesting and fun—and sometimes they are devastating. One moment you are totally clear about who you are, what you're doing, and where you're heading, and then out of nowhere something happens that turns everything upside down. Money problems erupt. A career move backfires. Your once good health takes a terrible turn. A relationship ends.

As much as we may wish it weren't so, change is one of the few constants in our lives. In fact, it's our resistance to change—and not change itself—that usually causes us the most distress. When we can accept that change is a natural (and yes, sometimes painful) part of life, we are in a much better position to accept it, to learn from it, and to evolve as a result of it.

As someone who has lived through the devastation of the failure of a business, loss of earnings, a debilitating illness, and the end of a relationship (once all at the same time), I can tell you with confidence that change, while painful, always comes bearing gifts. My own experience has taught me that the biggest, most dramatic changes are usually the ones that yield the biggest and best rewards. Today, I am grateful for the economic downturn of the early 1990s which devastated my business, because out of that experience came a career bigger, better, and more amazing than anything I could have ever planned for myself. My health scare placed me firmly on the path of healthy eating and regular exercise. And, of course, I am so grateful that the relationship I once believed would last forever ultimately crashed and burned, because if it hadn't, I wouldn't have been available to meet my beloved husband, Brian. Looking back, it's easy to see that some of the best things in my life today are a direct result of what I once judged as some of my worst times.

Lissa Coffey is a wise woman whose firsthand experience in the realm of change, closure, and relationships can skillfully guide you through times of transition. As you read this book you will begin to see not only that there is a light at the end of the tunnel, but that you have been drawn toward that light by design. If I had been fortunate enough to have stumbled upon the book you are now holding in your hands, I know my journey would have been easier, smoother, and quicker.

As you begin this process, allow your mind and heart to open to the new possibilities that this life change is urging you toward. I am willing to bet that something wonderful is about to happen.

With love,

Arielle Ford

Introduction

Each of us experiences some kind of loss in this lifetime. People come and go from our lives, whether by choice or circumstance. How we cope with these events affects how we move forward, how we see the world, and how we feel about our lives.

I'm not the only person to go through a divorce. When my first marriage ended after seventeen years, I thought I handled it well. It was an amicable parting, and we maintained a friendly relationship. Then, a few years later, my sister's husband died unexpectedly. My grief brought up new emotions, and I felt sad and angry and hurt as I relived the divorce in my mind. I realized through this experience that although I had moved on, I hadn't really gotten over it; I didn't have closure. I saw the parallels between my sister's loss and my own, and I actively sought to come up with a formula we both could use to alleviate our pain. From that research, and the discoveries that came out of it, this book was born.

Relationships take many forms: marriage, friendships, family, coworkers, classmates, lovers. Whenever two people have some type of a connection, a relationship is established. Our energy goes into these connections, along with our emotions, our hopes, and our human vulnerabilities. A relationship is an organism itself, and it can have a life cycle. But since a relationship is a spiritual organism, it doesn't die. It merely changes shape. The relationships we build with the people we encounter continue in spirit, in memories, and in lessons learned.

We are invested in our relationships with other people. We spend our time and emotions developing a bond with a person. We give of ourselves, through our love, our friendship, our concern, and our efforts.

When we are faced with what seems to be the "end" of a relationship, we may feel loss, grief, anger, or pain. We might even feel relief, or freedom. We may question the purpose for this change, whether it is abrupt or expected, and the necessity of it. The change may or may not be our choice or our desire, but something we must learn to live with. The uneasiness may nag at us for years as we struggle to understand. How do we get the "closure" that our hearts and minds so desperately seek, so that we can move forward with our lives?

We need to shift our perspective a bit when it comes to relationships. In our human form, we see the illusion of death and the ending of relationships. But what really takes place is a transformation. As we learn and grow through our relationships, they evolve. We can use this evolution as an opportunity for continued growth and personal transformation. The pains that we feel are growing pains. However a relationship changes—whether it is from physical death, a divorce, moving away, growing up, or due to a falling-out—we cannot only survive, but thrive, knowing that everything, always, is exactly the way it is meant to be.

How you use this book is up to you. It is divided into three sections. The first part deals with how our relationships come about, how we invest in them, and how they ultimately change. The second part is about what we do once the change occurs, how we handle it, and how we get over it. And the third part talks about how we move forward with our lives and this newly defined relationship.

At the end of each chapter I've included Transformation Applications. These are activities that you can do to help you process each of these stages and find the closure you need. It's a good idea to keep a journal a notepad, or a blank book for this purpose, so that you can write things down as they come to you, and look back over time and see how your perspective has changed.

I have also included Wisdom Affirmations. These are sentences that will be used to replace some of the negative thinking that can fill the mind. By repeating these affirmations, you will begin to see things from a new, more enlightened perspective. You'll think about your situation differently, and you'll feel better about it. If a particular affirmation resonates with you, write it on some sticky notes and post them on your computer, your bathroom mirror, your refrigerator door, or your dashboard—anywhere you will see the affirmation and be reminded of this higher wisdom.

This is the most personal book I've written. I've had a chance to learn from some of my relationships, and I share those experiences with you. I've also included stories from friends and people with whom I've worked. In some cases, I've changed the names of the people involved for privacy. One thing I've found from going through this whole process is that the anatomy of relationship is universal, and that there is a natural evolution of relationship. When we can look at the people in our lives as teachers or students, and as being there at a specific time for a specific purpose, then we value our relationships all the more. Life is all about relationships. It is about our relationship with our environment, with our Self, and with all the people in our lives and on this planet. There is so much we share.

A natural law works whether we are aware of it or not. It is a principle of nature that is in effect constantly, without favoritism. Gravity is an example of a natural law. It works the same for everyone, at all times. By being aware of gravity, we can move about more freely, with less risk of pain from falling down.

The Law of Relationship is twofold. It says:
1) We are all connected.
2) We are here to help each other learn and grow.

We are all connected in one way or another. We feel the same emotions; we share the same experiences. We are brothers and sisters on this planet. This connection bonds us and gives us a relationship with each other. A mother in any part the world can relate to another mother she has never seen because she knows what it means, and how it feels, to be a mother. We are all born the same way, and have to learn how to walk and talk and find our way in the world. We face challenges and heartache, no matter where, or how, we live. Our connection cannot be broken.

We learn and grow from our challenges and experiences. Our relationships bring us many challenges and experiences, and through our relationships we learn and grow. This is how we help each other. We may not even know that we are doing it, but just by being in a person's life, in some small way we are contributing to his or her learning process, as he or she is contributing to ours. Our actions affect other people in ways we can't even imagine. Even the times when we feel hurt by someone are an opportunity for us to learn and grow. We might not realize it at the moment, but in some strange and miraculous way, we are helping each other by going through this experience together.

My hope is that by reading *Closure* you will better understand how the law of relationship works, and that you will be able to find peace with yourselves and your lives in the present, no matter what happened in the past, or what happens in the future.

PART I

The Anatomy
of Relationship

Chapter 1:
Our Primary Relationship

Real increase of personality means consciousness of an enlargement that flows from inner sources.
—Carl G. Jung

In the Beginning

Before we are born into this physical world, and after the cells have formed to make us the human beings that we are, we are physically connected to our mothers. This connection feeds us, nourishes us, and helps us to grow until the body is able to sustain itself on its own. From the moment we emerge and that cord is cut, we are an individual, a separate entity. There is still a connection between child and mother, but it is unseen. There is a connection between child and father, mother and father, child and Universe, and between every living being. The connection between us is spiritual and profound, and yet subtle, so most of the time we are unaware of this tie that connects us to one another.

As we grow, we spend much of our time getting acquainted with the world around us. Everything is new; our senses are enlivened by each introduction to the unfamiliar. Or maybe it is that we are sensing something familiar and are perking up in recognition. In either case, our senses (sight, sound, smell, taste, and touch) are what connect us to the world, and we become more grounded, more rooted in this seeming reality the more we use them.

At some point, we learn that we have a name. We start to establish an identity. We attach ourselves to what is "mine," including our parents, our home, and our toys. We learn our address, and understand where we are supposed to be, where we belong. And somewhere on this continuum, and throughout our lives, we learn about ourselves. What tastes, smells, and sounds do we like? What makes us happy? What makes us cry? All of this information is filed in some system within our minds, so that when added together it makes up who we eventually think we are.

But are we that?

Who Am I?

We could, and probably do, spend a lifetime asking the question "Who am I?" and come up with dozens of different answers. And the answer we give when asked the question "Who are you?" may vary depending on the situation and the company. But the older we get, and the more experiences we have, the closer we get to the Truth. Who we are is that same baby that once was connected physically to its mother, and is still connected spiritually to everything and everyone in the Universe. Some things change: our size, our looks, our location, our age—and some things stay the same: our sweet spirit, our ever-present Self.

Since we are spending so much time with this Self, in this body, at this particular place and time, wouldn't it make sense for us to get acquainted? Growth is a process of learning who we are, who we really are. When we actively pursue this growth—through meditation, prayer, contemplation, study, or whatever means calls to us—then our awareness expands. We become more sensitive, more keenly aware of how we fit into the "big picture." We find our purpose, we experience our connections with others on a much deeper level, and we feel a sense of peace knowing that wherever we are, is exactly where we are meant to be at the time. It is all OK.

So it behooves us to develop this relationship with ourselves, because this relationship is the primary relationship in our lives. Everything around us will change. We will likely move to a different home more than once in our lives. On average, in the United States people move every five years. We will likely have more than one job in our lives, and maybe even more than a few different occupations. People will come and go from our lives, whether by our choice or theirs, by circumstances, or otherwise. But no matter where we go, what we do, or who comes with us, we have to live with ourselves. That never changes. Day and night, all our lives, this person—this spirit, this entity we are—is what we are, and where we are.

Getting to Know "Me"

Getting to know ourselves is probably the greatest challenge that we face. We don't realize it because we're so busy learning algebra, following the sports teams, watching the news, and making a living, among other things. But all the while the process continues. Sometimes we have "I" trouble—we can't see clearly. We get caught up in the many roles we play. Our lives are cluttered with duties and distractions so much that days, weeks, and months pass by before we can look up to see what's really going on. We focus on the minutiae of daily life and forget about the grandeur of life in general. How can we remind ourselves? How can we bring bliss into our field of vision so that we can focus properly on living rather than merely existing?

Growing up, I had the same insecurities a lot of girls do. I wore thick glasses. I had a big space between my two front teeth, and later had braces for almost two years. I had terrible allergies so I was always either sniffling or spaced out on allergy medicine. When I was in the third grade, my mom thought it would be cute to get mother/daughter pixie haircuts, so my hair was super short and I hated it. Growing it out was a nightmare, so I got a perm in the fourth grade, which was disastrous. I was very skinny and generally felt terrible about myself and my appearance much of the time. Thank goodness for Nancy Drew books—I immersed myself in that world! I had a couple of close friends and we would act out the stories in the books.

When I was in the fifth grade, my parents divorced and we moved. Then I felt even more different from the kids around me. New neighborhood, new house (much smaller), new school. On top of that, my mother went to work, so a lot of the responsibility at home fell to me, as the eldest of three. The divorce was not "friendly," so I felt like I had to take sides, and my already limited relationship with my father suffered. My father got custody of my little brother and the two of them moved to another city. At this point in my life, I knew myself as sad, abandoned, unworthy, even ugly. My mother used to try to console me with the story of the ugly duckling that turned out to be a swan. That didn't make me feel better; it made me feel as though my mother thought I was ugly too. It didn't help that my younger sister was beautiful and popular and ready for a bra before I was.

Somehow, I made friends with Catherine. She had a younger sister the same age as mine, and they invited us to join the girls' group at their church. It was Tuesday evenings after dinner. We'd all do craft projects, put on little skits, sing, and do some volunteering. I didn't really understand all of the religious aspects, but I got it that there was love in this place. I got it that I was accepted. I liked singing and praying, and the feeling of community. As I look back now, I realize that I was searching even then, and that this first experience helped put me on the spiritual path. My mother wrote out the Lord's Prayer and I clung to that piece of paper. It meant so much to me. I had a friend named Pilar who was Catholic, and I asked her to teach me the Hail Mary prayer. In some way, these rituals helped me to feel connected, to feel better, and to find a Self that I actually liked amid all the turmoil in my young life. I sought out spirituality. I asked for tarot cards and learned how to read them. I wore a Native American-style turquoise necklace and told everyone it was an amulet. I lit candles and sat in silence. This was my first experience with finding peace within myself despite all the chaos around me.

"Be Yourself!"

When we're young and preparing for an interview or some important presentation, the advice we get is "just be yourself!" But who is that? We don't really know yet. We're still figuring it out. A lot of times our parents or teachers try to help; sometimes they actually do help, but sometimes they just confuse us. Am I that insecure little girl with glasses? That's certainly not who I want to be! We can ask all kinds of questions. Am I the athlete my father wants me to be? Am I the class clown who gets into trouble all the time? Am I the "problem child" or "the smart one"? We search for ourselves through these labels; we learn about ourselves by what people say to us, and about us. Yet what we find is not our true Self, but a perception of a person based on our behavior, or on our appearance.

As time goes on, those labels change. I got contact lenses, the braces came off, and I learned how to wear makeup, so in college I grew out of my awkward stage. I became the social butterfly, the aspiring actress, the working student. Things change around us all the time. I graduated, got a job, got married, had kids. I was "the wife" and "Freddy's mom" and the neighbor, the song-writer, the grilled-cheese-sandwich maker.

All of these labels, all of these roles we play, identify what we do, not who we are. Who we are is so much more. Who we are is so far beyond what we see on the surface of our lives. And who we are remains the same, changeless, despite all that goes on with us on the outside. We are the Self that we find in silence. We are that pure and simple bliss that washes over us when we feel love. We are unlimited potential, freedom, awareness, and peace. And as much as we can read it and think it and know it, we don't allow ourselves to experience it nearly enough. We're so caught up in the "stuff" of our lives that we forget it, set it aside, discount it, or avoid it. And yet, here we are, all the time, waiting to be rediscovered. We don't really go anywhere. We don't really do anything. We simply are: beautiful, whole, complete, and perfect. Everything else is for our amusement, for us to experience so that we can learn more about ourselves. It's all part of the process. When we can truly understand this, we won't need to be so bothered by things that we think go "wrong." We can give up trying to control the details and really "go with the flow." We can enjoy the journey without anticipating an expected destination.

When we understand that our true Self never changes, we are comfortable with changing things around us. We understand that our "outside world" reflects our "inside world," and we embrace opportunities to make things different, or better, so that we "fit" more with our surroundings. Challenges are met with confidence, because we know that, no matter what happens, we're OK! When we decide to redecorate our home, change jobs, or reinvent ourselves completely, we feel free to express ourselves creatively. We're not as affected by criticism because we know who we are, and who exactly we have to please. We answer to ourselves, and follow our own instincts and intuition.

Reinvention

Reinvention is an amazing thing! It's one way for us to live many different lives in this one lifetime. There are several examples of people who have done just that. Madonna has made a career out of it—recording artist, actress, mother, author, icon—she is constantly evolving and experimenting with style.

My stepsister, Dorianne, went to the Julliard School of Music, and worked hard to earn herself a seat in the New York Symphony Orchestra as a violinist. Quite an accomplishment! She lived the life of a musician in the big city until she decided she wanted to experience a more lucrative career. So, she put herself through business school and moved to the West Coast, where she would be closer to her family. Dorianne ended up getting a job with a big corporation and moved up through the ranks to become one of its top executives. Meanwhile, she got married, had a child, got a divorce, and later remarried. The money was good with this company, but the demands and stresses of such a position left her with little energy for much outside of work. She decided she wanted to spend more time with her family, so she left her job and now is doing freelance work as a consultant. With an office at home, life is very different from how it was in the corporate world, but she feels that she has more balance, and this new situation better reflects who she wants to be and how she wants to spend her time. She even has time to play the violin again!

Sometimes we're forced into reinvention out of necessity. Another friend of mine, Lindsay, was a full-time stay-at-home mother with two little boys. She had put her career on hold when she got married and had children, and was very happy to devote herself to raising her sons. When she and her husband divorced, she needed to reenter the working world. Her experiences as a child growing up with dyslexia and as a counselor for troubled teens led her to a position as the vice principal of a high school for emotionally disturbed children. Now she supports herself, helps many teens who can really relate to her, and can still take her sons to their after-school activities. She also went out and got herself a truly great boyfriend, who is now her husband. Lindsay is a reminder to me that we decide what we want, and what we want to do. She created this new life for herself and she's very happy.

Where We Live – Literally and Figuratively

Reinvention might just be redefining ourselves on the outside. When I got divorced, my sons and I were still living in the house I had lived in with my ex-husband. We bought the house brand new a couple years after we got married. I was pregnant with our first son, Freddy, at the time. We watched it being built from the ground up, and would drive out to check the progress every weekend. The whole neighborhood was new, so there weren't even any streets for a while.

We moved in when Freddy was only a few months old, and the house was empty for a long time while we saved up money to buy furniture piece by piece. We picked out every tree and planted every blade of grass. As soon as we could build a fence, we got a dog.

Our best friends, Christine and Joe, were married in our living room! Then Brian was born and was christened in that same living room. I loved our home, and redecorated and remodeled it as the years went by. I put a lot of myself into it. It was my dream house in many ways.

So many memories in that house—birthday parties, family dinners, holidays, homework—all the daily activity that goes with life as it goes on and kids grow up. When we got divorced, my ex-husband got his own place close by and I stayed in the house so that the boys had the consistency of their same rooms and friends. It was definitely the right decision for our family at the time, and helped with the whole transition. But after four years I just couldn't stand it anymore. I had remarried and was ready to move on with my "new" life. I felt stuck being in that house. I felt like the past was so constantly in my present that I could not see the Self I was now. I finally realized that the only way I could move forward personally was to actually move out of the house. Thankfully, Greg, my new husband, understood, and we went looking.

We found a wonderful little house not too far away, and I knew that with a few little fixes, which I was happy to make, it would work out for us. The same day we had our offer accepted, I phoned my friend and real estate agent, Deborah, gave her a key, and the old house was officially for sale. The very next day we drove up to Monterey for a friend's wedding, and before we even got there Deborah called me on my cell phone to tell me that she had a buyer. She faxed an offer to our hotel and we sold the house for full price that night. That was the Universe working on our behalf to support our well-being. There were so many signs that this was the right thing to do. The couple that bought the house had twin boys and an older daughter. They had been looking for a long time and knew it was the perfect house for them when they saw it. I felt really good knowing that the house would be well loved. And I was especially happy when the twins agreed to take care of our box turtles so they could stay in the atrium of the house, instead of us trying to find homes for them!

I'd like to say everything was hunky-dory and life was blissful after that—but we weren't quite there yet. Freddy was going off to college, so the fact that we were moving didn't matter to him. But Brian was none too happy about the move. He had lived in that house his entire life, all sixteen years of it, and had never been one to seek change. On top of that, his best friend, Aaron, lived next door, and Aaron's house was his second home. Brian and Aaron were like brothers, so close they didn't even bother knocking—they just breezed in and out, back and forth, like the two homes were one. When the "sold" sign went up on our front lawn, Brian and Aaron kicked it down and ripped it up. The reality of the situation—that we were moving barely five miles away and that they'd both be driving in a few weeks—did little to console them. I don't think Brian had ever been so angry with me. He didn't understand that I just couldn't stay there anymore. He couldn't see things from my point of view. He was a bit irrational. At one point, I thought he would try to move in with the new owners!

I wanted to make our new home especially comfortable for Brian. I had Brian pick out the color of paint for his new room, and he chose a deep blue—definitely his color, not matching anything else in the house—but I didn't care if it was what he wanted. And when we moved in, Aaron and Brian's other buddies were there to help him arrange his furniture. They all thought the place was "sweet." Brian grumbled for a few days, but settled in, and before long his friends were hanging out here quite a bit. School started and Brian ran for junior class representative. He had never done anything like that before; it was a real leap in putting himself out there. And he won! Pretty soon there were kids in our driveway painting the homecoming float. Our house became the meeting spot whenever his friends went out because it was closest to the school.

Later that year, Brian had to write an essay for school about an event in his life and how it had changed him. He wrote about moving. He wrote that, as much as he didn't want to move, he was glad that he had. He said that he had learned that change can be good, and that you can grow from it. He explained how it gave him confidence and allowed him to stretch his boundaries, so that he was able to meet new people and have new experiences. And now, since he had proved to himself that he could do this successfully, he was more prepared to go away to college, and actually looking forward to more changes in his life.

Wow!

As a mom, I was grateful that I followed my instinct, and was so proud that Brian was able to articulate just what a positive the move had turned out to be for him. I had wanted to move so that I could put myself in surroundings that better reflected my life and what I wanted it to look like. What ended up happening was that Brian was able to find more of himself in the new place too. To me, that was just miraculous.

"A Rose By Any Other Name..."

A name is a tool we use for people to identify us. Another way we can choose to reinvent ourselves is by changing our name. The names we are given at birth are typically chosen by our parents. We may or may not feel like that particular name represents who we are, or the image we want to present to the world. Freddy's dad and I named our first son Frederick Jack, after both of our grandfathers. Frederick may have been a popular name in the 1800s, but in 1986 there weren't many Freddys around. That's one reason why I really liked the name, as there were several Mikes, Matts, Jasons, and Jareds to be had in his preschool class.

Freddy, in finding his identity, took on a few different personas when he was very young. One time I had a landscaper working in our yard, and Freddy struck up a conversation. Freddy was very talkative and made friends easily. The two seemed to be enjoying themselves so I went about getting lunch together in the kitchen. When the landscaper finished, he commented on how smart Freddy was. And he said, "And what an unusual name he has!" I explained that he was named after our grandfathers, and the man said, "Really! Your grandfather is named Raphael?" I couldn't help but laugh. Freddy had renamed himself after a Ninja Turtle.

I guess it didn't stick, because one day Freddy came home with a school work sheet with the name Logan on it. I thought he had gotten his paper mixed up with another child's. But he told me no, he wanted to be Logan now. Evidently, this was because Wolverine, the character in the Marvel X-Men comic books, is named Logan. This name lasted a little longer. I still have a binder of trading cards that is labeled "Logan's Cards."

When Freddy was born we joined The Fred Society. Fred Daniel, the "Head Fred," started this group for people named Fred. He's got great T-shirts and items for sale on his Web site, as well as wonderful stories about Freds all over the world, famous and otherwise. When Freddy was in the first grade, we were invited to a taping of Leeza Gibbons' television show. A bunch of Freds went and they all wore their Fred T-shirts. The topic of the show was "What's In a Name?" and Leeza interviewed Fred Daniel about how he started the group. Then she asked my Freddy—who, at about six years old, stood out as the youngest in the group—"So, what's it like being named Fred?" She put the microphone right up to his face, and he smiled really big and said, "I used to not like it, but now I like it," and the audience burst into applause. Freddy was so happy! He didn't change his name again after that. I thought as he got older that he would prefer to be Fred rather than Freddy, but he says Freddy suits him, and all of his friends seem to agree. Remember when child star Ricky Schroeder grew up and, wanting to be taken more seriously as an actor, changed his first name to Rick? That was his way of re-inventing, or redefining, himself. And yet Donny Osmond is still Donny after all these years. Whenever I call Freddy's cell phone, his message says, "Hey, man, it's The Fred! Leave a message!" So now, maybe he's "The Fred" as well.

I have a good friend named Max. I was surprised to learn from Max's father that Max's given name is not Max. I have no idea what his parents named him when he was born, but he chose the name Max for himself and that's how he is known. When he was about four years old, he was riding in the car with his dad and saw one of the gauges on the dashboard that read "MIN" and "MAX," and he asked his dad what that meant. His father explained that "MAX" meant the most, the highest amount. And right then and there, the little boy declared Max to be his new name. This little boy knew, even at that young age, who he was and how he wanted to present himself. Max was so tenacious about it that his name stuck!

My grandmother was named Elise, but everyone called her Penny. She got the nickname when she was young and a popular song was "Pennies from Heaven." One of her boyfriends thought she looked "as pretty as a penny." The name suited her, and although she never changed it legally, she went by Penny all the time.

I've changed my name a few times. I was born Lisa Marie Granich. I didn't really use my middle name much. When I got married at age twenty-two, I took my husband's name and became Lisa Nelson. I know women have the choice to change their names or not when they get married; actually, men have the same choice. Some people feel that they don't want to "lose their identity" by changing their name. But to me, it's just a name—just an arrangement of letters. I didn't have any big career or reputation built up then and I liked the idea of that particular tradition, of being Mr. and Mrs. Nelson. I thought it was romantic. When I started my company, I began using my middle name because there are so many other Lisa Nelsons out there, so all of my songs and books had my full name on them, Lisa Marie Nelson.

Then, after seventeen years as a Nelson, I got divorced. When I remarried, I already had two books, several CDs, and a couple of videos out under the name Nelson, but I was ready for a fresh start with this new marriage. I felt that changing my name was making a big commitment, and I chose to do it. There were other benefits too. First of all, I really like the name Coffey and all the creative connotations I can play with. As for my books, I would be shelved right between two of my favorite authors: Deepak Chopra and Alan Cohen. Bonus! So I became Lisa Marie Coffey, and I knew somehow it would all work out just fine.

A couple of years after I got married, I was working on our dosha yoga DVD and met a musicologist and numerologist from India, Dr. Harre Harren. He wrote healing music for each dosha specifically for our DVD, and we spent a lot of time communicating back and forth. Hemalayaa (note the two a's), who was then Hemalaya Behl, was our yoga instructor on the video, and she had Harre do her numerology. She told me she was changing the spelling of her first name, and using only that one name professionally. I thought that was really interesting, so I had Harre do my numerology too. It's quite a process. He looks at your name and your birthday, and comes up with various formulas; it's all very mathematical. He offered me a few different options, some of which wouldn't have been practical, and I chose to go with Lissa Coffey. Harre gave me all the reasons why this name would work out better for me, and I decided to just embrace it. After all, I wrote all about Vedic philosophy, and I loved the whole Ayurvedic lifestyle, so I thought I might as well really live it in every way. And I felt very good about my "new" name from the moment I wrote it—it felt right. I ran in to tell Greg, my husband, and he just smiled at me. He knows me so well that nothing surprises him anymore.

Actors often change their names. John Wayne was originally Marion Morrison. Cary Grant was born Archibald Leach. And Lauren Bacall was Betty Joan Perske. Susan Weaver changed her first name to Sigourney after a character in *The Great Gatsby*. Singers, musicians, and authors frequently change their names too. Anyone can. Alicia Cook would have been a great name for a food network star, but the beautiful singer and pianist chose to change her name to Alicia Keys. And we all know that Samuel Clemens wrote under the now very famous name of Mark Twain. The idea is that the outer persona reflects the strength and confidence we feel within. A name change doesn't change who we are, it just helps us to project who we are more easily.

Self-Expression

There are so many ways we can change the "outer" Self. We express ourselves with the clothes we wear, our hairstyles, even our bodies. We can change our clothes with our moods. We can put on makeup and it washes off. Some people love tattoos as a form of self-expression. Some people spend hours in the gym to get great muscles and toned bodies. It's a choice. I'm all for looking good, but I wonder what it is really saying about ourselves when we try too hard to be "perfect." Do we really want fake teeth, fake hair, fake nails, fake tans, false eyelashes, colored contacts, plastic surgery, and so on? It's one thing to be groomed and presentable; it's another to go overboard and try to be someone we're not. But every one of us has to determine that for ourselves. We have to look at what makes us authentic, and real. A test would be—do you know who you are, and love who you are, without all the accoutrements? Do you love yourself naked? It comes back to "be yourself." Be the best "you" that you can be. Be true to who you really are.

We express ourselves all the time, in a variety of ways. We do so with our words, and with the work we do. We express ourselves every day with how we live our lives, and how we treat other people. And, most importantly, how we treat our Self. We need to take care of ourselves: body, mind, and spirit. The body is a vessel to carry us through this life, so that we can have the opportunities we need to learn and grow and experience.

A New You

A lot of time reinvention comes about because we get to know ourselves better. We discover something new or different about ourselves, something we like and want to express. Our eyes are opened a bit to the potential within. We're not so much "new" as "more" of the person we really are, who is there all the time. Sometimes, the process of self-discovery is intense. It can come about as a result of something that happens to us, whether it's difficult or wonderful. We might not even recognize what we're going through at the time, but as we process the experience, we get closer to ourselves.

There are many life events I can look back on and say that I learned more about myself from them. Certainly the whole experience of childbirth and parenting was huge, and I continue to learn from my children. I also learn quite a bit from traveling. My trip to India had a profound effect on me. This came at a time when I was at something of a crossroads in my life. My marriage was almost nonexistent and had been for a long time. I was exhausted from struggling with a child with special needs. The stress I was under was manifesting in various physical ailments. I was feeling lost, not knowing what I should do, or even what my options were. I knew I had to get back to myself somehow. So, when the opportunity came up for a group trip to India with Deepak Chopra and my Chopra Center friends, I decided to go.

This was very uncharacteristic of me. I don't like flying at all, so the thought of twenty-some hours in the air and switching flights twice was very scary. I didn't even have a passport, because other than a couple of quick trips to Mexico I'd never left the country before. But I knew I had to go. I just knew it. Something in me compelled me to go. I fought it and tried to rationalize all the reasons why I shouldn't go. But in the end, I figured if I was ever going to go to India at any time in my life, this was it. I was researching Ayurveda for my book, *What's Your Dosha, Baby?* and knew that I could learn more in India than anywhere. I also felt safe and comfortable knowing I'd be with a group of people I knew already. My then husband had no desire to go. But Freddy did, and my good friend Janie was taking her son who was the same age, so Freddy came along to experience India too.

Before I left, I kept having really weird dreams. I thought it was just my subconscious bringing up fears and dealing with them. There was one recurring dream where I had a baby. To me, this was almost a nightmare—I already had two sons, I didn't like being pregnant, and I didn't want any more children. But in my dreams I kept having a baby, a little girl. I wondered if some part of me wanted a girl, since I had two boys. I didn't know what it meant. And I was too busy packing to try to figure it out!

From the moment I stepped off the plane, I felt like a different person. I felt free, unburdened by my usual routine. This was such an adventure, and I loved every single moment of it. We meditated at least two hours a day. We did yoga, listened to amazing lectures, toured the temples, and ate delicious vegan food. I had time to myself, time to think without all of the responsibilities I had at home.

One day, Janie and I were out shopping with the boys and we met an Indian psychic. This man read palms, and we jumped at the chance for a reading. I sat next to him, he took my hand in his, and a big smile spread across his face. "You're pregnant!" he declared. My mouth fell open as I flashed back to my dreams. I wasn't sure I had heard him correctly. And I knew it was physically impossible to be fact. "Oh," he said, "don't worry, this is wonderful. You are pregnant with your Self! You are going through big changes, and you are about to give birth to your Self." It took a while to sink in, but I knew he was onto something—that dark-haired baby in my dreams was me. It started to make sense.

One morning, while Deepak was leading us on a guided meditation, I sat in silence and asked for a sign. What should I do? How should I handle things when I got home? What was right for me and my family? And then I heard Deepak's voice continuing with the meditation, saying, "Step into the realm of uncertainty, this is where there are infinite possibilities." I felt like the Universe was speaking to me. The timing of that statement couldn't have been more perfect. The "known" to me was my unhappy marriage. The "unknown" was what life would be like as a single mother. I had been clinging to the known out of fear of the unknown. But now I knew I had to be brave, to be true to my Self and make some changes. I couldn't compromise or make excuses anymore. When I got home my husband and I talked, and although we had discussed divorce before, we agreed that this was finally it. I think he was relieved too, because we had been in this place of trying and coexisting for far too long. We both wanted something more. Still, after being together for twenty years, our entire adult lives, it was extremely difficult. But it was right for both of us.

That's how growth is. It's difficult. Childbirth is physically painful for both parent and child. Growing up is hard. We have to learn to speak and to express ourselves. There are times we don't know what to say, or how to say it. We have to learn to walk. We fall down a lot, and get bumps and bruises. We get growing pains. We mess up and suffer the consequences. But we also learn from our experiences, whether we interpret those experiences as good or bad at the time. Learning about our Self is a lifelong process. And one of the most important ways we learn is through our relationships.

Notes:

Transformation Applications

- How well do you know yourself?
- Ask yourself this question: Who am I?
- Make a list of all the roles you play in your life.
- What is your name? Your nickname? What name do you want to go by?
- Make a list of words that people would use to describe you.
- Make a list of words that you would use to describe yourself.
- How do you define yourself?
- What do you love to do?
- What makes your heart sing?
- List your favorite: music, movies, colors, foods, causes, weather, words, places, times, etc.
- If you had a month free of your usual responsibilities and an unlimited amount of money, how would you spend your time?
- Research ways to get to know "you," such as:
  Enneagram (www.enneagraminstitute.com)
  Astrology, either Western or Eastern (Jyotish)
  Numerology
  Personality Tests (www.youniverse.com)

Wisdom Affirmations for Our Primary Relationship

- I am whole, complete, and perfect, imperfections and all.
- I am aware of my inherent value, and I give myself the care and attention I need to maintain perfect health—mentally, emotionally, physically, and spiritually.
- I am capable and competent, and I create my reality with the choices I make.

Chapter 2:
Establishing Relationships

To a large degree "reality" is whatever the people who are around at the time agree to.

—Milton H. Miller

We Can Relate

So here we are. We know we're not alone in this world. We see people everywhere we go. Unless we choose to live as a hermit, we are bound to have some relationships in our lives. This is not only natural, it is essential to our well-being. The word "relation" dates back to the 1390s and its original meaning is "bringing back, restoring." A ship is a vessel, a means of transportation. A relation-ship is one way to bring us back, to restore us, to remind us of who we really are. In the 1950s the word "relate" came to mean "to feel connected, or sympathetic to." A relationship is a physical illustration of our connection with each other.

Family Ties

We are born into some relationships. The family is just the first of the many connections we will establish during our lifetime. The dynamics that occur during our youth set the stage for how we handle other relationships as we go along our way. We are observers as well as participants. How Mom treated Dad, how Dad treated us, all of the daily interactions and conversations get stored away in a kind of mental file that sets up expectations about how we think relationships are defined. Sometimes this works for us, and other times it takes years to change our perception into one in which the type of relationships we truly desire can thrive.

My father grew up in a household where the husband had a job outside the home and the wife basically did all the work taking care of the house and kids. His mother cooked and cleaned and did laundry and dishes with no help at all. When my dad married my mom, he just assumed that's the way it would be in his household too. He expected my mom to be happy doing everything all by herself. He figured he was making the money, so he was entitled to golf on the weekends. But that wasn't my mother's idea of a marriage. She was lonely and stressed, and she ended up getting depressed. There is no fault or blame, just a major lack of communication. They did not come to a consensus, or an understanding, of what their marriage would be like before they got into it.

To avoid things like this, we need to establish our expectations and express our needs and wants early on in any relationship. We have to know what we're getting into with this other person. We need to be clear so that we understand each other's vision of what a relationship is. We might not want to pursue a relationship if our expectations are dramatically different. If our visions are too far apart, there may not be a way to bring them together—and it is better to know this up front. There are some things we are willing to compromise on, and other things that may be deal breakers. But how do you know what's going on in someone else's head unless you actually talk about it?

My parents divorced when I was ten years old. My former husband's parents divorced when he was about the same age. One of the reasons we stayed married for so long and worked so hard on our marriage is that we didn't want our children to go through the experiences we did when we were young. And it's also the reason we tried very hard to make the divorce amicable, and the transition an easy one for our kids.

Relationships at their best are real-ationships; real meaning honest, open, and true. When two people come together with this understanding, that each can be himself or herself and be valued and accepted exactly as he or she is, that is the basis for a real-ationship. With the family, it seems like we have no choice. We're related by blood or marriage, and for some reason we've entered into the Universe with this particular brood. There are lessons to be learned from these people! There is some purpose to this, even if it is beyond our current human understanding. We're thrown together because we have something to learn from each other. Be open to it.

Siblings

My younger sister, Marci, younger brother, Billy, and I were very close when we were young. We had the same parents and lived in the same house, so we understood to some extent what we were each going through. A few years after our parents' divorce, my brother went to live with my father, and then the two of them moved hours away, so my sister and I didn't get to see either of them very often. I think it was harder being away from my brother because we felt like we were missing out on a big part of his life. He wasn't at school with us. We didn't know his friends. We didn't know how he spent his time. Even though he was the annoying little brother, we missed having him around. We are lucky that now, as adults, we all live in the same general area, and are able to see each other and participate in each other's lives.

In high school, my sister and I got a little competitive. We were both very outgoing, so at times there was some tension when one or the other got more attention. Now, I can look back and see that we were both starved for the attention we weren't getting from our parents, so we tried desperately to receive it from our peers. I ran for every student council office, was in all the school plays, and worked on the school yearbook and newspaper. My sister played volleyball and was the consummate socialite. As much as we needed each other, we didn't want to need each other, so we fought. A lot. We were very territorial with what few possessions and clothing we had.

When I went off to UCLA I got some perspective on things. I experienced being on my own and could define myself as something other than "Marci's sister." I came back home for Christmas and my sister was geared up for another round. I took her aside and we had a heart-to-heart talk. I explained to her that I wanted to be her sister and her friend too. Our parents had sort of set us up by labeling her "the pretty one" and me "the smart one." They always said Marci would get married first because she had all the boyfriends. Or that I would get into the better college because I was so smart. I told her that there was no reason to compete, or to compare ourselves to each other. I knew she was smart too— and that I was pretty. I was done feeling inferior and I didn't want her to feel that way either. We didn't have to be defined by our parents. She got it. Totally. We established a brand-new relationship that day. We hugged and cried, and we've been best friends ever since. Marci is always there for me, no matter what. And I am always there for her. We have been through a lot together over the years.

Making Friends

As we grow up and go to school, our social circle expands. Our parents may set up playdates, and we begin to make friends. As kids it's easy; we have no expectations, so we aren't afraid to put ourselves out there. But then we start to attach ourselves to things, and we aren't as eager to share. We start to get a sense of territory and hierarchy. This pretty much peaks in middle school, when raging hormones get the best of us with bullies and mean girls. Cliques form, and we get segmented into groups. We become concerned about social status and popularity. We feel analyzed and criticized, and a lot of that pressure comes from ourselves. Yet somehow we survive it. As adults, if we had to go back and live with the stresses these young teens face I don't think we could do it. There's a built-in emotional resiliency that we lose with age as we get more comfortable in our safe surroundings. But the upside is that we also become more compassionate and caring people.

I missed my ten-year high school reunion because I was busy giving birth to Brian. So, when my twenty-year reunion came around, I was really eager to go and see the people from my high school class again. Of course I wanted to connect with my old friends, but I also was curious about what everyone else had been up to after all these years. I sort of expected the old cliques to form again; that people would stick to their familiar roles. But that's not what happened at all. Everyone talked with everyone. People who never even said hello to each other in high school were deep in conversation. You couldn't see the cliques at all. Naturally, I couldn't even recognize some of the people anymore, so that may have been a part of it. It was almost as if we were all in costume, dressed up as older people! But with age comes some wisdom and some mellowing, and a lot of the "posturing" just drops away, and we come to this point where we are not afraid to be who we are, or to show the world who we are. I came across one couple and was surprised to see them together. I said, "I didn't know you knew each other!" And Don said, "We didn't really know each other in high school. We got reacquainted at the ten-year reunion and have gotten married since then. Now we have two kids!" Isn't that wonderful?

Friendship

Some people come into our lives and we end up developing a friendship. We choose our friends. Or our friends choose us. It's some sort of mutual agreement that takes place, sometimes without our even being aware of it. It starts with an attraction. We see something in this person that we like. And then it builds with a connection—we find that we have something in common. We can talk to this person, or laugh with this person, and we are at ease with this person.

With certain friends I have had over the years, I can remember the exact moment we met. I was in the first grade when I met my very first best friend, Kim. We were in Miss Eaton's class learning to read. Miss Eaton passed out some books to the class and told us to read them, and said to come up and get the next one when we were done. Kim and I were the first ones to finish, and we made eye contact on the way to the teacher's desk. Then, we finished the second book and practically bumped into each other on the way to pick up the next book. By the time we had read the third book, we just looked up and smiled at each other—instant connection. We were best buddies.

I met my friend Carolyn at Kim's birthday slumber party in the sixth grade. Even though I haven't talked with Kim in decades, I still remember that her birthday is December 15! My family had moved, so I was at a different school, but Kim and I stayed in touch. There were several girls at the party and we broke up into small groups to put on skits for each other. I ended up doing a skit about a mechanical Santa Claus that had Carolyn in stitches! How can you not like someone who thinks you are hilariously funny? We became fast friends, and when we went to the same middle school the following year we could see each other all the time.

What both Kim and Carolyn gave me at that time in my life was confidence. And I badly needed it. Because of them, I took more challenging classes. I pushed myself harder. They saw things in me that, due to my home life, I couldn't see in myself.

We meet the people we meet for a reason, and it is always interesting to discover what this reason is. Sometimes the reason reveals itself right away, and sometimes it takes years to unfold. It could be a karmic relationship, one in which one person, or both, is meant to help the other learn or grow in some way. We feel a kind of chemistry in relationships like this, a sort of "meant to be" connection, as if we've known this person for a long time, even though we've only just met. Pay attention when these feelings arise, because they signal that this is an important relationship. Karmic doesn't necessarily mean good or bad, just important, or meaningful.

I was ushering at church one day when I met my friend Lindsay. It was her first visit, so I was the first person to greet her. Even though I had never seen her before, I knew she was going to be my friend. She came up to me, and my first impression was that she was tall and beautiful and radiating joy. She asked me about the service, and afterward she sought me out and we talked some more. We connected easily since we both were the mothers of two boys, though hers are much younger than mine, and we arranged to get together at my house. There are so many amazing qualities that I see in Lindsay. I love that she's spiritual, and open-minded, and full of energy. She has really become my soul sister. I appreciate that I can truly be myself with Lindsay. She doesn't judge me, or expect anything from me. It's really easy to be her friend. Through Lindsay I met Barbara, who is also a wonderful friend. And it's interesting how all of our lives and experiences have both paralleled and intertwined through the years. We have helped and supported each other through some major life events.

Our relationships act as a mirror for us to learn more about ourselves. If there is something we find particularly attractive in someone, it is because that quality is somewhere in us; that's how we recognize it. The same holds true if we see something we dislike about someone. Somewhere that same quality lies inside of us. Rather than hide it away, it serves us to look at it without judgment, see where it comes from, and figure out what we want to do with it.

Karma

A lot of times, "love at first sight" is really karmic recognition. We see someone, or meet someone, and it feels familiar, as if we already know that person. And we may have known him or her in a past life, or on some spiritual plane. In spirit, we make arrangements with people to meet again for some specific purpose—for something we need to learn, or clear up with each other. Or it may be that our purpose with each other was left unfulfilled the last time around, and here we are again trying to get it right.

I heard one of my favorite actresses, the late Natalie Wood, talk about seeing her future husband, Robert Wagner, for the first time. She was a young girl, walking the back lot of the studio holding her mother's hand. Robert Wagner walked by and she turned and pointed at him, telling her mother, "That's the man I'm going to marry!" That interview made a big impression on me. I loved that she knew, without hesitation, that he was to be in her future. And he was! I always thought something like that would happen to me, and I would just know. And it did.

It was my sophomore year at UCLA. I was in a sorority and there was a dance marathon for charity, held in the Ackerman Ballroom. I was dancing with one of my fraternity friends and we'd been going for nearly ten hours straight. My hair was in pigtails, all my makeup had melted off, and I was tired and definitely not at my "freshest." Out of the corner of my eye I saw this guy walk in. He looked like Tom Selleck, who was pretty much the hottest guy on TV at the time. Super tall, dark curly hair, a mustache—this was 1980, so mustaches were cool then—and he was wearing a letterman's jacket. The first thought that popped into my head was, *That's the man I'm going to marry*. Seriously! It hit me really hard.

I then went into strategy mode. I had to find out who he was and how I could meet him. I started asking others on the dance floor if they knew him. I didn't want him to leave without finding out his name. I didn't want to approach him myself because I was not exactly looking my best and I so wanted to make a good first impression. Finally, I found my friend Larry and asked him about this guy. Larry said, "Oh, that's Jeff, he's the president of our fraternity. Do you want to meet him?" I was a little flustered, and explained to Larry that while I really wanted to meet Jeff, now wasn't a good time. At the time, I was working as a waitress at Acapulco's restaurant in Westwood, so I told Larry to have Jeff come by there some Saturday so that I could meet him. Turned out to be a good strategy. That Saturday was Valentine's Day, and I was working, looking cute in my little off-the-shoulder ruffled blouse. I was in the bar, and Jeff came in, walked right up to me and said, "I'm looking for Lisa." It was so busy that night, and I was rushing from table to table, but I managed some small talk. I ended up apologizing and explaining that while I normally didn't give out my phone number, I'd like him to call me sometime. Feeling rather tacky, I scrawled my name and number on a cocktail napkin and he was on his way. It was a bit awkward, and I wasn't sure if he'd call, but he did. And we arranged a date for dinner.

I told the girls at my sorority because I was so excited. They gave me the rundown—if he's serious about you, he'll take you to the Charthouse. That was the "it" place, where all the girls went for big dates, to get pinned or engaged. I'd never been there before, so this was the first I'd heard of it. I knew they were onto something when Jeff took me there for our first date. We talked about everything—our backgrounds, our families, our goals. We were together from that night on. Months later, he even gave me his fraternity pin, which was a very big deal. He eventually took me to dinner at the Charthouse again, and proposed. A year later we were married.

It's easy to establish relationships when you follow your instincts. A smile goes a long way, as does an open heart. I followed my instincts when I saw Jeff. He followed his instincts when Larry told him about me. The

Universe sets up signposts for us, and when we pay attention we don't have to hesitate. To me, Valentine's Day was a sign, and the Charthouse was a sign. The signal my body was giving me in terms of butterflies was a big sign! How could I not pay attention?

I never thought I would experience anything like that again. But twenty years later, the butterflies came back. I certainly was not looking for a relationship—that was probably the last thing on my mind. I was taking a class at the Chopra Center and I noticed this incredibly handsome man sitting in the row behind me. My heart skipped a beat. I knew this meant something. It was a little more than I was ready to handle, so I avoided him the whole long weekend, until the last night, when we were seated next to each other at dinner. We couldn't stop talking and laughing; it was so comfortable and sweet. I really enjoyed his company. Since he was from Australia, I really didn't consider it anything more than that. When he asked me if I had a sister, I knew he was attracted to me too. Somehow, the Universe conspired to bring us together, overcoming all obstacles and covering two continents, because Greg is now my husband.

All of life is love, and love is all about relationships. There are many different types of love, like the love of chocolate, the love of reading, the love we feel for a pet, or the love we have for our own child. Then there is the friendship kind of love, the romantic kind of love, and the love we feel for nature, Spirit, God, or whatever name we choose to call the energy that connects us all. But it is all love. We live in love. We just don't always realize it.

Connecting

I write an online advice column, and one of the things I hear most frequently from people is how difficult it is to meet people and to make friends. They ask where they can go, what they can do, to make these connections. As human beings we crave that personal contact and conversation. It can seem like a daunting task to establish new relationships when you're new to an area and don't know anyone. Or to let others know you're "available" if you've returned to the dating scene after a long time. In any case, the solution is the same: you've got to put yourself out there. You have to take the initiative and find ways and places to connect. Here are some suggestions:

Join a club. The whole purpose behind professional groups like Kiwanis, Rotary, Optimists, and Toastmasters is to network. Networking means meeting people for business reasons, and it can also mean making friends. When we first moved to Woodland Hills, Jeff and I joined the local Toastmasters Club. We both had an interest in public speaking and it gave us something to do together. We ended up making lifelong friends with another couple, Jake and Eileen. And we improved our speaking skills too! The great thing about these professional groups is that they often have mixers so that people can get to know each other. And you can join clubs within the clubs by volunteering for committees and organizing various functions with a smaller group of people who share your same interests.

You can find clubs just about anywhere you go. If you go to church, there are often women's groups, singles' groups, dinner clubs, or study groups you can join. The community center often has groups for seniors, teenagers, and single parents. The public library or local bookstore often has book clubs or reading groups. If you have kids, join the PTA, the "Mothers of Multiples" Club, or be the room parent for your child's class. That way, you can connect with other parents who have kids the same age as yours. If you like to participate in sports, find a league and join a team.

Volunteer. Every community has opportunities to contribute. What is your passion? Where do you want to help? You may be able to find a local chapter of The Sierra Club or Habitat for Humanity. You may want to spend time at the animal shelter or pet adoption agency. There are chapters of the American Red Cross, Big Brothers Big Sisters, UNICEF, the United Way, and countless other charities all over the world. Choose a cause that speaks to your heart. Volunteering is a wonderful way to meet like-minded people. I met some amazing women when I was a member of the Los Angeles chapter of Childhelp USA, which helps abused and neglected children. We had monthly luncheon meetings and an annual gala. It was a lot of fun, raising money for a worthy cause. But the part I liked best was that we also had the chance to connect with the children we were helping. There was a type of "friend" program where we could be matched up with a child and spend time with him or her, so we could really see where our efforts were making a difference in the lives of these children.

When my boys left for college, I had a little more time on my hands, and I decided to volunteer at a local group home for foster children. I came in on Sunday evenings to cook dinner with the teen girls. I bonded with one of the girls, and I am now her Big Sister through the Big Brothers Big Sisters program. I love my Little Sister, and for me this is a lifelong relationship. I can't imagine my life without her.

Take a class. When we were younger and went to school every day it was easy to meet people. We were all sort of in the same boat, and oftentimes we got through the stuff we didn't like about school because we had our friends there to support us. But now it's our choice to be in school, to take a class and learn something we really want to learn. And we can still make friends. We can share notes and help each other study. Being in a class together is something we automatically have in common, so the ice is already broken. Learning brings so much to our lives. Think about what makes you curious, what challenges you, what you want to conquer. It can be a new language, a skill, a sport, something that will help you in your career, or something just for fun. It can be a one-day seminar or a weekly evening class. Besides the friends you make, you'll gain newfound knowledge, and probably have a lot of fun too.

Travel. When you take a group tour, you're really not traveling alone. All of the stops are planned, so there's less stress, and you have time to meet people and get to know them. You might even end up having travel buddies you see on a regular basis when you go on trips together.

Go online. The Internet has opened up the world to us! There are hundreds of social networking sites now, where you can meet people from all over the globe. Within each network are groups, discussion boards, and other opportunities to make friends. They are easy to navigate, and you can find groups where you can share your knowledge and learn about things you're really interested in alongside like-minded people. We can meet people we otherwise never would have had the chance to meet. And we can reconnect with people from the past, even look up an old high school friend. Because of the Internet, there are no borders anymore, no limits. We have access to all kinds of information, and we can reach people anywhere, anytime. Set up a profile, post a photo of yourself. If you like to read, you might be interested in GoodReads.com, which is like an online book club. If you're interested in things such as meditation or yoga, you might enjoy the community at Intent.com. I blog there; look for me, and you can be my friend!

Socialize. We need to say "yes" more often. Too many times, we find our comfort zone and resist breaking out of it. The known can be comfortable because we know what to expect. The unknown can make us nervous—but that's a good thing! We expand our boundaries, we challenge ourselves, and we meet new people. So go to those parties, or have a party yourself. Through people you meet people. Have a picnic in the park and ask everyone to bring someone you haven't met before.

Work. This is where we go every day. Even if we work at home, we don't work in a vacuum; we see people on a regular basis at the post office or the office supply store. The working world is a great place to meet people. Smile. Introduce yourself. Do your best work.

Remember that in an office you're part of a team; it's an ensemble, and you are needed and appreciated for what you can bring to the table. You're there because you have something to contribute. Work is one way that we express ourselves, and it's one way through which people can get to know us.

Notes:

Transformation Applications

- Make a list of people you know.
- How many are friends?
- How did you meet? Where? When?
- Who would you like to get to know better?
- If you were having a party, with unlimited resources, who would you invite? Where would it be held? What activities and entertainment would you provide?
- What qualities do you value in a friend?
- What qualities do you bring to a friendship?
- What relationships do you want to bring into your life?
- Where can you go to establish new relationships?
- What can you do to establish new relationships?

Wisdom Affirmations for
Establishing Relationships

- I am connected to every single person in this world in some way.
- I see myself in other people.
- My heart is open to embrace the people and circumstances that come my way, knowing that there is a purpose in everything.

Chapter 3:
Building Relationships

Each friend represents a world in us, a world possibly not born until they arrive, and it is only by this meeting that a new world is born.

—Anais Nin

Friends and Others

We come across lots of people during the span of a lifetime. There are those we pass on the street, or share an elevator ride with, or sit next to on a plane. And then there are those we actually meet and establish a relationship with. Many relationships don't go beyond being established. We have many "acquaintances," situations we find ourselves in where we may know the person's name, but we don't really know the person. We could live next door to someone for years and not get beyond the obligatory wave at the mailbox. In order to get to know a person we need to build a relationship.

There's an old saying that the best way to have a friend is to be a friend. Of course, there are all types of friends. On Facebook and other social networking sites we can accumulate hundreds of "friends," who then we just breeze by on the Internet. But a good friend, a real friend, is invaluable. The kind of friend who will take your call in the middle of the night, the kind of friend who will bring you soup when you're sick—those are the ones we remember always. Those are the relationships we cherish. And they don't happen automatically, we have to work to cultivate them. Whether it's a friendship, a family relationship, or a love relationship, the process of building the relationship is the same.

Getting to Know "You"

Some people are masters at small talk. Set them loose at a cocktail party and they can schmooze with anyone! Conversation doesn't come so easily for many of us. Yet, we know how important it can be to make a good first impression. Conversation is a social skill that can be learned, and it can definitely help us to build relationships.

The most important thing to remember about conversation is that it is an exchange of information. That means while one person talks, the other person listens. Sounds easy, right? Not always. Conversation is an art. And you can get good at it by practicing. Start with the listening part. I took an acting class once where we had to partner with someone we didn't know, and one person had to talk while the other listened. Then, we had to repeat the story we were told to confirm that we had really heard it and understood it. We had to look into that person's eyes as he or she was talking to really take in the information, to feel what he or she was feeling. Interestingly enough, when we were in marriage counseling, Jeff and I had to go through a very similar exercise. It was good to have that third party there to coach us on a very fundamental skill that gets pushed aside when two people with strong opinions are trying to influence one another.

In acting, you need to hear what the person is saying so that you know how to respond. If you don't listen and you just say your lines, then there is a disconnect—the characters aren't relating and the words don't make sense. It's the same in real life. If you're really listening, then you aren't busy thinking about what you'll say next. You're looking at the person and taking in the information, so that you can form a response based on what was communicated.

Listening is important. We all need to feel heard. We talk because we have something to say. We don't like having to repeat ourselves in an attempt to get through to a person. It is so frustrating when our conversations go around in circles and we feel like we're talking to a wall. When we get the feedback that we are heard, and understood, we feel good, validated.

Communication doesn't take place just in words. We can say one thing and mean another. We have to take into account body language, tone of voice, and all the emotions that come through. When people say, "I'm not angry!" and they're tense, they have their arms crossed, and are shaking their head, what are they really saying? Probably something along the lines of "I'm angry, but I don't want you to think I'm angry because I need to be in control right now." If you don't understand what someone is saying, or his or her body language gives you a different impression, ask for clarification.

Asking questions is a great way to get to know someone. They don't need to be probing, personal questions, just questions that show you are interested. To be an interesting person, all you have to do is to *be interested* in the person you are talking with. And share some information about yourself, as well, so that it is a conversation rather than an interview. Engage. Respond. Exchange. Relate. This is how we learn about each other, and get to know each other.

The amazing thing is that when we really know someone well, when we've built up that relationship, we almost have our own language. We don't need to say anything; we can just sit in silence and be totally comfortable with each other.

Availability

One of the keys to being a good conversationalist is being present. This means paying attention to the person you are talking with, listening, and being open to wherever the discussion takes you. Being present in a relationship means being available. It doesn't matter how far away you live; you don't have to be face-to-face. It can be as simple as returning phone calls, checking in by e-mail, or lending an ear (or a shoulder) when it is needed.

When my brother was in high school, he lived with my dad and I was off at college. We hardly ever saw each other. But when he went to college, he chose to come to Southern California, where I was living and working. He reached out to me, and that meant a lot to me. Right away we started building a relationship. I was there for Billy as a big sister, having him over for dinner and showing him around. He was there for me as a brother, helping me when my car wouldn't start, and taking me out to lunch when I was pregnant and stuck at home. We knew we could count on each other, and we started to bond, more so that we ever did as kids. Now we're both busy with our work and friends, and we don't see each other very often. But I still know that if I need Billy, all I have to do is call and he'll come running.

My friend Carolyn lives in Boston, and I hardly ever get to see her. But every time we talk, or get together, it's like no time has gone by at all. We don't need to be in constant touch to know that we are there for each other. We have this unspoken mutual agreement. We've seen each other grow up, and have been through too much together to let it fade away. When we were young, we were practically inseparable; we saw or talked to each other every single day. We spent a lot of time building the relationship, talking late into the night about boys and diets, riding our bikes to each other's houses, shopping for cute clothes and dreaming about the future. We even shared a locker, and Carolyn starred in one of my theatre shows. There's something about those trying and sometimes terrible teen years where a friend can be a lifeline. We helped each other through broken hearts and hormones and college applications. We ended up going to different parts of the country for college, but we always stayed in touch with each other. Our relationship has changed, and maintaining it is easy in its new form. Now we're inseparable in a totally different way. Even with kids, husbands, and jobs that take up lots of time and attention, we are still friends. We have a bond that doesn't go away. We're in each other's thoughts, and that's really nice to know.

Lindsay and I check in with each other every few days. It could just be a quick text message, a long catching-up phone call, or a leisurely "ladies" lunch. Not because we have to, but because we want to. I helped her move into her apartment after her divorce. She came over and took care of Brian when he was sick and I had an important meeting to attend. We built our friendship and now we're in maintenance mode.

When I think of famous BFFs (Best Friends Forever, in textspeak), I think of Oprah Winfrey and Gayle King. Oprah is godmother to Gayle's children. As busy as these two dynamic women are, they talk every day. How did they meet? Here's what Oprah had to say on XM Radio: "When I was twenty-two years old and working as a TV anchor in Baltimore, there was a young production assistant in the newsroom, Gayle King. One night there was a snowstorm and she couldn't get home. I said, 'Hey, you can spend the night at my house.' She said, 'I don't have any panties.' I said, 'Well, I do. I have clean panties, and once I give 'em to you, you don't have to give 'em back.'" Now, that's a way to build a friendship! What I love about this story is that the bar was set right away. They basically declared that they were there to help each other, no matter what the other one needed. And that's what their relationship is like even after all these years. In her magazine, *O*, for which Gayle is an editor, Oprah wrote: "Something about this relationship feels otherworldly to me, like it was designed by a power and a hand greater than my own. Whatever this friendship is, it's been a very fun ride."

Kindness

A little kindness goes a long way in building a relationship. It's the small favors you do for people. Bringing in the mail when they're on vacation. Picking up some fresh strawberries for them when you come across a bargain. Driving them to get their car after it's been serviced. It can also include contributing to their charity when they are fund-raising. Or remembering an important day for them, like a birthday or anniversary.

Kindness can also mean being nonjudgmental. It's not telling the other person what he or she should or should not do, but respecting his or her choices. It's accepting people for who they are, and not trying to change them in any way. Judgment is toxic to a relationship. It just doesn't feel good, so a healthy relationship can't be sustained. Kindness is nurturing, sweet, soft, and loving. That's an environment in which a healthy relationship can thrive. If you want to be friends with someone, you have to be nice to him or her. It's that simple.

Be the Dog

Years ago, when Marci started a new job—her dream job at the time—she met with a lot of resistance at her office. I called to check on her after a few days to see how it was going. She was miserable. She said that although she loved the work, and knew she could really contribute, she felt like the other people in the office didn't like her. They had already formed their little cliques and she felt like an outsider. She was very uncomfortable with this situation and was having a hard time functioning in that kind of an environment.

The advice I gave her was this: "Be the dog." Basically, the people in her office were acting like cats. When Marci came into the room, they would toss their tails in the air and walk in the other direction, arch their backs, or even hiss. Rather than to try to be a cat and fit in with this group, she needed to take a vastly different approach. She needed to be the dog. She needed to bounce into the room with her tail wagging, full of energy and with a big smile on her face. That's how a dog is. A dog isn't aloof. He doesn't wait for you to be his friend; he assumes you already are his friend! He approaches with enthusiasm. I told Marci to take on this attitude and see what happened.

Sure enough, in a few days the whole energy around the office shifted. How could anyone not accept a happy and loving dog? She had all those cats purring! Once she had built up positive relationships with her coworkers, she was able to work more efficiently and effectively. It was a better working environment for everyone.

Give-and-take

What do you have to offer in a relationship? What can someone learn from you? What experiences can you share with someone? A relationship is give-and-take. You learn from a person and he or she learns from you. Be open to learn, be open to new opportunities, and share yourself and your knowledge with people. In relationships, we learn about the other person, but we also learn about ourselves. We're exposed to new situations and circumstances, and we can see how we are, how we like doing something, and can find new abilities and interests.

Allow people to give to you. So many of us are very comfortable giving, but are uncomfortable receiving. Allowing someone to give to you is a gift in itself. We learn from giving. It is a wonderful experience to be able to give. So say yes, thank you! And when you give, do so without expectation. Give from the kindness of your heart, not from the expectation of receiving something in return. Give because you want to, not because you want something back.

Thank You

Showing appreciation and gratitude is another important way to build a relationship. Every one of us wants to feel that we are appreciated, that our efforts are noticed. When we don't feel appreciated, we feel taken advantage of, or taken for granted. Showing appreciation can be as simple as saying "thank you." Notice when someone does something nice for you and express your gratitude. When people show you appreciation, it feels good, and it makes you want to do more for them! When there is reciprocation, then a friendship is being formed.

Trust

An important component in building relationships is trust. If we feel we can trust someone, we are more likely to open up and talk about ourselves. We don't worry that whatever we say is going to end up on the

Internet somewhere! It takes awhile to earn someone's trust. We may start out tentatively and see how it goes. For example, you set a lunch date—a certain time and place. When you both show up, you begin to believe that you can trust each other to do what you say you're going to do. It's a start.

Throughout my first marriage, I saw signs that our relationship was not a priority to Jeff. But I chose to ignore them, or make excuses for them. When we had an appointment to talk with the pastor for our prewedding counseling, he was more than half an hour late. I had to sit there with the pastor and assure him that Jeff really did want to get married and was merely running late. He also was late for the wedding rehearsal. Everyone else was there—all the bridesmaids and groomsmen, both sets of parents—but no groom. Eventually he came in, full of apologies, saying he had had an important work appointment.

Since that's how we built our relationship, that's pretty much the pattern that was set. He put work first. That was his priority, and either he assumed I was OK with it or he didn't care what I thought. When I was pregnant and got very sick, I couldn't get in touch with him, so my sister ended up leaving work and driving clear across the city to take me to the emergency room. When I was in labor with Brian, he left my side to drive to his office and fax a proposal. After my second miscarriage, he dropped me off at home and went back to work. These were times in my life when I really needed the love and support of a husband, and he didn't provide it. I couldn't trust him to be there for me in that way. I knew he had it in him, because he could always manage to be there for his father and brother. I wanted so badly to trust him, and for the relationship to work out, but looking back I can see that we were doomed from the start, because that trust between us was never built up in the first place.

Definitions

At some point during the building process, there comes a time to define the relationship. In romance, that often means having "the talk." Can we talk about us? Where is this relationship going? What do I mean to you? It is time to get on the same page, to understand just what each person wants and needs out of the relationship. Are we in love, or just friends? You need to find some mutual agreement in order to continue the relationship. Otherwise, if one person wants more and the other just can't give it, there's not much of a future there.

With friendship it works much the same way, except that the person with the lesser commitment, or lesser investment in the relationship, ends up leading how the relationship is defined. For example, one person would love to be best friends, eat dinner at each other's houses, and exchange holiday gifts, but the other person simply isn't available or willing to give that much time or energy to the relationship. The first person is left with what the other one is willing to give, and has the option of enjoying the relationship on those terms. We can have several friends, so chances are there are others who are more than willing to fill that gap. But in romance, when you're looking for "the one" and your needs aren't being met, then it's time to move on.

Joe and Carlton were pledge brothers at a UCLA fraternity. When you live together, socialize together, and go to school together, it's easy to get to know each other. They were fast friends. Carlton's sister, Christine, used to come to the fraternity house to visit her brother and go to some of the parties there. Christine and Joe got to be good friends too. The three of them hung out and spent lots of time together during the years they were in school. Then, Christine and Joe realized they really liked spending time with each other, just the two of them. A lot. The definition of their relationship changed. Built on a strong foundation of friendship, romance blossomed. Now they're married with two kids.

Relationships are fluid; we move closer and further apart, depending on what else is going on in our lives. Relationships that have been built with trust will adapt with the inevitable changes that arise.

Notes:

Transformation Applications

- Practice "Be the dog." How does this help you to feel more comfortable in a group setting? What reactions do you get from people?

- How available are you to friends? Family? People in general? How do you communicate with people? How do you stay in touch?

- Time is the most valuable gift you can give. Where do you give your time? How much time do you "waste" doing things that don't add value to your life? How can you make time to spend with people?

- Write thank-you notes to people in your life—just for the sake of thanking them.

- Be mindful of promises you make. Keep your word. Have integrity.

- Define for yourself how to keep balance in a relationship.

Wisdom Affirmations for
Building Relationships

- I am here to share myself and my unique talents with other people.
- I am always learning and growing, and I am receptive to the experiences that people have to share with me.
- As I get to know people, I get to know more about myself.

Chapter 4:
Maintaining Relationships

Friends share all things.

—Pythagoras

Intimacy

Many people would say that the key to a good, long-lasting relationship is communication. But there is so much more to it than that. In Vedic philosophy, intimacy is a result of the combination of truth and time. Intimacy is that closeness we all crave in a love relationship, when you can really be yourself with a person, and are completely comfortable in every way. You feel as though that person "gets" you—and you love and cherish that person as well. Intimacy has been broken down to mean "into-me-see." It's that unabashed authenticity that is so wonderful when it is shared. But how do we get there? And how do we maintain the relationships that we have built?

Truth

First, let's look at the element of truth. Going beyond communication, to really being honest with each other. Sure, you're talking. But are you truly being honest? Are you really sharing your true Self? What is it that you are not saying that is getting in the way of your relationship?

If you are hiding money, lying about debt, or keeping secrets about your finances from your significant other, then you are being dishonest. You are committing financial infidelity.

We live in a materialistic society. We are consumers. We have easy access to money—with ATMs on every corner, credit card offers filling up our mailboxes, and online shopping twenty-four/seven. We have more ways to get and spend money than ever before. And because of this, consumer debt, excluding mortgages, has doubled in the past decade. It now averages close to twenty thousand dollars per household. And this is a huge issue in marriages.

Since we are marrying at a later age these days, we come into the relationship with our own monetary histories, just as we come in with our own sexual pasts. Most adults—67 percent of women and 74 percent of men—enter marriage with at least some debt from cars loans, credit cards, student loans, etc. Are we up front and open with our partners about our assets and debts? Do we know what we're getting into when we commit our life, and our finances, to this other person? Marriage is as much a promise of fiscal partnership as of sexual monogamy. We need to talk about money, get it out in the open, make sure our values mesh, and come to agreements about spending and saving. Set common goals and work toward them together. We need to get away from "mine" and "yours" and think of money as "ours." Couples who have this team approach to finances have a higher rate of success in staying together. It's OK to have separate accounts, but it's not OK to hide that money. The other person needs to be aware of it.

Couples argue about money more than any other issue. And those arguments are more intense than when we talk about any other topic. Money is tied to our hopes and dreams, our sense of security, and our emotions and expectations. When you're married, the world treats you as one financial entity, so you need to approach finances honestly. One person can't operate purely out of self-interest.

Financial infidelity can have legal and long-lasting consequences, but it also takes an emotional toll on couples. It's a breach of trust. One partner is keeping secrets, and the other feels betrayed, asking, "What else are you not telling me?" This leads to a decrease in emotional intimacy, because one partner is so afraid of that secret coming out that he or she can't let down his or her guard and be himself or herself. If trust is lost in one area, it is more likely to be lost in other areas as well. Both partners need to feel that they can talk freely, and they need a sense of security about the future. With financial infidelity you lose that. Just as with sexual affairs, you have to work hard to rebuild that trust.

Time

The other element in the equation is time. We need to spend time with each other to have an intimate relationship. And yet, where do we spend the bulk of our time? Work. When we have a chance to spend time outside of work, we have choices. We can choose to hole up with our computer at home, go out with friends, work on our hobbies, visit our relatives...or spend time with our significant other. One of the reasons my first marriage ran its course was that we didn't spend time together. Jeff traveled a lot. He was always gone, on the road, selling or speaking. Meanwhile, I was at home with the kids. When he got back, I couldn't wait to go out. But there weren't many activities that we both enjoyed doing together. So we ended up doing everything separately, got used to it, and grew apart.

It is important to make time to maintain our relationships. Family and group activities are always good, but one-on-one time is essential to keep a relationship healthy. If you have kids, that can mean sending them to a friend's house so you can have alone time with your spouse. Go for a walk. Take a class together, something like dancing or cooking where you're working as a team. Have date nights, or date weekends away.

With children it's important to have one-on-one time too. I used to schedule "dates" with my boys, where I'd take just one of them to lunch, or dinner and a movie, or shopping, and we could really talk about what was happening in their lives. This time was so precious to me, and even though they're basically grown, Freddy and Brian still like to ask me out on a "date" when they come home.

Sometimes, it's nice to just be together and not do anything. You can just share the same space, be in the same room, and not have to talk. You can each be doing your own thing, but feel close because you're together.

We need to spend time with our friends and relatives too. How much time depends on the two of you, and how much you feel you need. My friend Michele lives a few hours away, so we end up spending more of our time online or on the phone when we connect. My dad is pretty happy staying at home, but he loves it when I come over just to visit.

Three Things

Vedic philosophy says that there are three things we can give our children so that we have a strong relationship with them: attention, affection, and time. We can apply this to all of our relationships. By spending time with a person, it shows that he or she is worthy of your time and energy. It shows that you care enough to choose to spend your time with that person. Time is the most valuable gift we can give other people. Attention means you know what is happening in their lives. You pay attention to how they're feeling, you're there to listen, and you're available when they need you. Doing small favors is another way to show that you are paying attention to their needs. Affection is that endearment we all need so much—kind words, hugs, smiles. Greet them warmly when they walk in a room. Show that you are happy to see them.

Sex

We can have sex without intimacy, and we can have intimacy without sex. A 2003 *Newsweek* study found that 15 to 20 percent of couples in the United States make love no more than ten times a year. There are many reasons why libido may be low, such as hormonal changes, stress, illness, and fatigue. And this is fine as long as you maintain intimacy, and are both in agreement as to your physical needs. It is also possible for a relationship to have deteriorated to the point where intimacy is lacking, which affects both the quantity and quality of sexual activity. We need to feel close to our partner; we need that emotional intimacy in order to fully express ourselves physically. The less we make love, the less we feel the need to, and new habits form that are hard to break. It's a downward spiral. If we can maintain intimacy with our partner on every level, then our sex lives will be the better for it too.

Foreplay takes place all day, not just in the bedroom. Connecting with your partner via a sweet e-mail, greeting him or her with a kiss, sharing meaningful conversation at dinner, holding hands while watching TV—all this can be considered foreplay. If your schedules aren't jibing so that you have enough alone time together, make an appointment to spend time with each other. You'll be glad you did.

And time together after sex is important too. We've just allowed ourselves to be very vulnerable. Most of us want to hear three things: "I love you," "You are wonderful," and "I am all yours." It helps us feel safe and loved.

Interdependence

The best relationships are interdependent. Dependent or codependent relationships, where one person needs the other person to need him or her, are toxic. With independent relationships, there is a lot of freedom, but there is a lack of connection. Interdependent relationships are those where people know that they are whole and complete, regardless of any relationship they are in. They know that they bring something to the relationship, and that they also benefit from it. They function as people and as a couple. In relationships like these, the whole is greater than the sum of the parts. This is the case where one plus one equals more than two. In this case, two committed people can help each other, support each other, and accomplish more together than they could individually. You are who you are, and you are able to express that. You don't "lose your identity" by being part of a couple.

Equanimity

Relationships aren't always fifty/fifty. It's nice when they average out to be that though. Most of the time, one person is pulling more weight than the other. For a while it might be a ninety/ten relationship, then seventy/thirty, then thirty/seventy. A fluctuation occurs that is organically based on what is happening in each other's lives. And that's great—as long as you both know what's going on and can pick up the slack when you need to, knowing that you may be the slacker at some point in the future. What you want to strive for is balance. If you were playing on a teeter-totter and were stuck with the board being straight across, it wouldn't be any fun at all. The ups and downs give us some momentum. Sometimes we have to do the pushing, and other times we can enjoy the ride. It's nice to be cared for, and it's also nice to be the nurturer. How great is it to come home from work to a ready-made dinner? Or to have a warm bath drawn for you when you're sore from working out? Those are things we can do for each other. Those are the perks of being in a relationship. And those are the kinds of things that help to make a relationship last.

It Takes Two

There's an old saying that it takes two to tango. Yes, indeed. We need to remember that the next time we get in an argument with someone. Instead of fighting, we need to use our communication skills and our social skills, and really work to find a solution instead of trying so hard to be right. Would you rather be right or happy? We can all get along. When expressing yourself in a heated discussion, there's no need to bring up things that happened in the past. The past is over! Now is the only time there is; be in the moment. Maintain calm and use a calm tone of voice. If things look like they're getting out of control, agree to step back and reconvene at a specific time. Give yourselves time to cool off and think more clearly. Stick to the issue at hand. Don't attack or insult the person; that won't get your anywhere. And don't threaten, or guilt trip, or use emotional blackmail to get what you want. What you really want is for both of you to be happy!

See things from the other person's point of view. Stand in his or her shoes for a few minutes. Pretend you are him or her, and really get a grip on why he or she feels so strongly about this. When you change your perspective, the view shifts. You're not so much thinking about "me" as you are "us," and that's an important distinction.

Apologies

If you discover you've done something wrong, or something you regret, or if you have hurt someone's feelings, apologize! Take responsibility for your actions. Don't play the victim. I remember so many times as a kid, having a fight with my mother and being so mad and crying, and just knowing she was wrong and wishing she'd come in and apologize. And many times, she did! That meant so much to me. I remembered that with my own children, and I have never been afraid to apologize to them. It doesn't take any of your power or control away; it doesn't make you weak. It actually shows that you are strong enough to learn from your mistakes. It shows that you care more about the other person than about winning an argument. Those two words, "I'm sorry," may just be the two most beautiful words ever spoken when it comes to healing a relationship.

Jonathan Alpert, M.A., licensed psychotherapist and advice columnist, explains why apologies are important in relationships:

Apologies are important because they show humility and an acceptance of responsibility. It also shows that the person has the ability to reflect on a situation and improve. This growth is crucial for a healthy relationship. The best apologies are those that are heartfelt and sincere. Anything short might be perceived as being said out of obligation or for selfish reasons. Apologies should be specific and cite the incident/behavior and the effect it may have had on the other person (I'm sorry for X and how it may have made you feel). It should also address, at least subtly, what the person has learned or will change. Once an apology is given and accepted it's important for the recipient to view the person through a fresh lens, not the old one.

Just as important as it is to apologize it is important to forgive and accept. To not forgive means the person is likely holding a grudge. The purpose of this is to protect. With a grudge there's anger. The anger energizes a person, providing an illusion of control, and protects the vulnerabilities of the person. As long as one is angry they aren't going to get hurt. This is the mind's way of protecting one from re-experiencing the situation. To accept an apology may render the other person vulnerable and the recipient may feel he/she let the person off the hook too easily. Accepting an apology is powerful, however, due to the aforementioned, not always easily done. To help, imagine you're packing for trip and you can only bring essential items. Would you include items such as a positive attitude, sense of humor, and good food, or resentment, anger, and bad food? Lighten the load and take only what's beneficial.

Criticism

Many arguments come about because a person feels criticized. How many times has that been justified with "I'm just being honest"? There's a way to be honest and still be kind. Words can be weapons, or words can be instruments of peace. We need to use our words carefully. We need to be sensitive to a person's feelings, especially when it comes to his or her ideas and creativity. Creative people identify with their creations. Their work is an extension of themselves. They take it personally if you don't like something they have created. And at times, saying nothing is just as bad as saying something negative because they will assume the worst! So find something to compliment. Direct your comments to the person, rather than the creation. You can say, "You're so talented!" You don't have to say, "That sweater you knit is really ugly."

One of the worst fights Greg and I ever had was after we moved into our new house. I spent weeks decorating to make it beautiful and comfortable, taking into account Vastu and Feng Shui and both of our personal tastes. I was so excited when the last chair finally arrived after being reupholstered. I dragged Greg out of his office, where he was likely deep in thought and focused on something terribly important, and pulled him into the family room, practically jumping up and down and clapping my hands. "What do you think?!" I said proudly, and eagerly awaited what I thought would be his equally enthusiastic reply. "I don't like it," he grumbled, and promptly went back to his office and shut the door. My heart sank. I followed him, knowing that this was probably not the best time, but thinking that I could possibly make him see the light and give me some glimmer of delight. "What do you mean, you don't like it? How can you not like it? It's beautiful! It's perfect!" I stood there, flabbergasted. He looked up calmly and said, "You always told me to be honest, and I'm being honest."

To make a long story short, our discussion went on for the rest of the day, until we came to the understanding. When one of us makes an effort in some project for the family, and the other one makes no effort, the other one does not have the right to disapprove. And to remember that Greg is color-blind, so Lissa is in charge of all things related to color, including decorating. And that when one person says, "What do you think?" when a project is finished, it really means, "Tell me you love it!" And we also agreed that the time to offer opinions is before the work is done, not after. This works both ways. I have learned not to make critical comments about the stock market because that's Greg's territory and I really don't understand it anyway. I trust him to make the decisions he feels are best.

With most disagreements it is best to remember what is really important. The relationship is important. Being happy is important. Everything else is just "details." Focus on what matters most, and know that once this issue goes away, whatever it is, you still want to have your relationship.

The "getting to know you" process is ongoing in a relationship. As people, we learn and grow all the time, so we change, and the relationship changes as a result. The relationship we may be maintaining today may not be the same relationship we got into when we first got together. If we can shift and adjust and work it out, then the relationship can thrive.

Zen

In Buddhist philosophy, we learn that the ultimate goal is not unity, it is harmony. We don't all sing the same song, or even sing in the same key, but we can learn to make beautiful music together. We can appreciate each other's uniqueness, each other's voice, and harmonize.

Another way to look at conflicts in a relationship is with the Buddhist philosophy about suffering. You can ask, "Will this action increase suffering, or decrease suffering?" The goal is to decrease suffering. If you ask this question, and surmise that taking an action, or saying something, will increase your partner's suffering, then don't do it! Strive for harmony in the relationship; strive to decrease suffering, which will in turn increase happiness. Will washing the dishes increase suffering or decrease suffering? Well, it may temporarily increase your suffering if it's something you don't want to do. But look at the big picture. It will decrease the suffering of your partner because he or she won't have to wash the dishes. And his or her happiness will bring harmony to the household, and allow you two to spend more time together. Ah! See how that works?

The Mirror

Our relationships act as a mirror for us. If there is something we really like about a person, chances are that it is something we embody, something we also like about ourselves. If there is something we dislike about a person, it is likely that it is something we also identify in ourselves, whether or not we want to admit it. Our relationships challenge us. They're not always easy, but that's how we learn and grow. We learn about each other, but most importantly, we learn about ourselves. The people in our lives are our teachers. They are a mirror, holding up to us what we need to look at.

Before we get angry or react, we can look in that mirror and pause. "What is it about this situation that I can change? How can I change my perspective to see the lesson in this?" When something gets us riled, it is more often than not about ourselves, and not about the other person. Instead of accusing and blaming and directing our focus on everything that person did "wrong," we need to look at ourselves, and the part we play in this scenario. We can't change another person, but we can change ourselves. We certainly can change our thinking and our perspective. In the book *A Course in Miracles* one of the lessons says: "I am never upset for the reason I think." Look more deeply, find the lesson, and learn from it.

Show You Care

It's important in any relationship to show that you care. It's true that little things mean a lot. Know your partner's favorite drink so that you can order it for him or her when you go out. Be sensitive to a friend's dietary needs so that you can make a meal for him or her that he or she can actually eat. Brian's friend Aaron is gluten-intolerant, so I always make sure that we have gluten-free snacks for when he comes to visit. And when we have Aaron over for dinner, I am careful to serve foods that he can eat and therefore enjoy the meal along with the rest of us. Lindsay loves my special Chai, so I make it for her when she comes to visit. My mom has Greg over for a vegetarian dinner when I go out of town. Food can feed our soul as well as our tummy!

Greg knows that I get cold at night, so he turns on the electric blanket to warm up the bed for me before I get in. Michele clips magazine articles she thinks I will be interested in and mails them to me. These little gestures go a long way in making me feel loved and appreciated.

Nicknames and secret "love codes" are another way to show you care. Greg says that when he first saw me I was wearing a headband and I reminded him of Snow White, so that's his pet name for me: Snow White, or SW for short. I promptly dubbed him my Prince Charming, or PC. Many of our notes back and forth are from SW to PC, and vice versa. It's sort of our own secret code. In love relationships, nicknames like honey, cupcake, and sugar abound because love is sweet and absolutely delicious! Code can be unspoken too. When my boys were little we had a secret "I love you" code. I'd squeeze their hands three times for "I love you," and they'd squeeze back twice for "me too!"

Respect

When asked about the secret to the longevity of their relationship, long-time marrieds often say "respect." Having respect for each other is essential in any healthy relationship. The first way to show respect is to respect yourself. Take care of yourself. Keep up with the grooming. Shower or bathe daily. Brush your teeth twice a day. These seem like such obvious and simple things to do, but at least once a month there's a letter to an advice columnist in the paper where one of the spouses is complaining that the other is basically being a slob. She goes around in tacky sweats, or he's stopped shaving; either way, they've "let themselves go." That's a surefire way to diminish someone's respect for you.

When we dress up for ourselves, it shows self-respect. When we dress up for our relationship, we are demonstrating in an outward way that the person in our life is worthy of our time and effort. It shows that we feel that we are worthy of respect, of a loving relationship. Now that's a turn-on! We don't need to do anything fancy, just look nice and smell good.

Another way we can show respect in our relationships is to be polite, to have manners. That's what etiquette is all about, being conscious of others around you. Chew with your mouth closed. Excuse yourself when you burp. Say "please" and "thank you." I've spent a long time teaching my boys what it means to be gentlemen. They know to hold doors open, to offer a seat to an older person, to put napkins on their laps when eating, to help bring in and put away the groceries. I think the people in their lives, whether girlfriends or roommates or in-laws, will appreciate that they have integrated these good habits into their lifestyles. Little thoughtful gestures help to maintain strong relationships.

Encouragement

We can encourage our friends and support them in their dreams and endeavors. We can be cheerleaders, rooting for them! And we can be coaches, helping them to stay on track. We can help each other achieve. It helps to have someone there to say, "You can do it! Keep going!" and also to say, "It's OK, I'm here for you, no matter what happens." When we know we've got someone in our corner who believes in us, it helps us to summon the courage to really go for it.

We can also encourage each other in our spiritual growth. We can meditate or pray together, read and study together, attend classes or church together. We don't have to practice the same religion, but we can share the beauty and rituals of our spiritual practices with each other. In Vedic philosophy, our relationships are a tool through which we can grow spiritually, a way we can find our true Self, to remember who we really are. When we can share this experience with another person it is absolutely beautiful, precious, and perfect.

Love "As Is"

Ayurveda is India's five-thousand-year-old "Science of Life." It is the art of living in harmony with nature. And it explains the nature of everything in the Universe, including our relationships.

Ayurveda explains that everything in the Universe is made up of the five elements: air, space, fire, water, and earth. From these elements come our three doshas, or mind/body types: Vata, Pitta, and Kapha. Because we have all five elements in our physiology, we each have all three of the doshas too, just in different proportions. Because we are unique individuals, one or two of these doshas will be dominant, expressing through us to make up who we are and how we tick. When we know our dosha, we learn more about ourselves, and how to take care of ourselves. The idea is that when we are in balance, we are our healthiest and happiest.

Vata is made up of air and space. In nature, Vata shows up in a stalk of bamboo or a birch tree. We also see Vata in a hummingbird or a gazelle. People who are Vata dominant typically look long and lean. They may be tall or short, but they have long limbs, and you can often see their bony knees or elbows. Celebrities who are Vata types include Jim Carrey, Uma Thurman, and Will Smith. Vata types are very creative—think Quentin Tarantino and Steven Spielberg. In fact, you'll find lots of Vata types in the entertainment business, as they thrive in creative careers. Vata types can be visionaries, like Barack Obama.

Vatas get cold easily, so they need to keep their environment warm. They also have a difficult time traveling; too much air and space is an excess of Vata and they get nauseous. To help prevent this, they can sip warm ginger tea on the plane, sweetened with a little brown sugar. Vatas have sensitive digestion, so they need to eat warm, cooked foods. They don't have much of a reserve in which to store their energy, so they need to get lots of sleep and keep to a routine. They shouldn't overdo it mentally or physically, or they'll get worn-out. Exercises like yoga, walking, and dancing are sufficient for Vatas. They get bored easily and have a short attention span. Many times, what looks like attention deficit disorder is really a Vata imbalance.

Pitta is made up of fire and water. We see Pitta in a pine tree—strong and ambitious, reaching toward the sky. Pitta is represented in animals by an eagle or a tiger. These animals don't waste their energy, they go after what they want and get it. Pitta types are more muscular or athletic in their body type. And mentally they are thinkers, and are natural leaders. Because of the fire, you often see a redness to the Pittas' hair or skin. Pitta celebrities include Donald Trump, Madonna, and Brad Pitt. Many professional athletes and politicians are Pittas, as they excel in those fields. Andre Agassi and Hillary Clinton are just two examples.

Pittas get hot easily. This can manifest as hot in temperature, or hot in anger. Pittas need to stay cool to be in balance and at their best. They have a strong digestive fire, so they can eat raw foods and cool foods. They need to avoid foods that are spicy, as those give them too much fire. Cooling foods like mint, cucumber, and coconut can be great for Pittas. They are good businesspeople, but can be workaholics, so they need to make sure they get enough fun and play in their lives to balance out their intensity. They tend to like competitive sports.

Kapha is made up of water and earth. Kapha shows up in nature in an oak tree, grounded and with deep roots. Kapha animals include the serene swan or the strong elephant. Kaphas are mellow, easygoing, friendly, and sweet. Physically, they can look a little heavy. They tend to have dark, thick hair, and big eyes and lips. Kaphas are generally beautiful—think George Clooney, Angelina Jolie, and Beyonce. They have soft skin and long eyelashes or thick eyebrows. Kaphas are very loving, and they make good teachers, parents, and doctors. They also have a strong bent toward the philanthropic. They want to help people, and they make loyal friends.

Because Kaphas can gain weight easily, they need to exercise a lot! They should be running, lifting weights, breaking a sweat every day. When out of balance, Kaphas can get depressed and lethargic. They need motivating. Spicy foods are good for Kaphas. Foods they need to avoid include red meat, dairy products, and fried foods. But Kaphas have a sweet tooth, and they love to eat, so keeping them out of the kitchen is a chore!

Remember that we all have some of each dosha in us; it is just that one dosha is dominant. For example, Oprah Winfrey is the quintessential Kapha type: thick dark hair, big eyes, beautiful skin. She is loving, philanthropic, loyal, and prone to weight gain. Oprah is also an amazing businesswoman, which is evidence of the Pitta in her. And she is creative, having won acclaim for her acting performance in the movie *The Color Purple*. Creativity is a Vata quality.

When you know about the doshas, you know about your nature, and the nature of other people. This helps us in every area of our lives, including our relationships. We learn to be more accepting of people, understanding that they are the way they are for a reason. We learn to love what is, rather than what we think should be. We would never expect a tiger to be anything other than a tiger. We wouldn't say, "Hey, tiger, start acting like a swan!" We love and appreciate the tiger for exactly who he is. We also know that there are ways we can help the tiger to be the best tiger he can be. We can be better partners, parents, friends, employers, and employees when we apply this ancient wisdom to our relationships.

Vata types make friends easily and change friends often. They are less likely to feel attached, and move on more freely, although they are prone to anxiety. They see the "big picture" and any drama (even if they create it) as temporary Vata types respond most to touch and sound. To calm a Vata, use warmth, hugs, massage, and gentle music or soft words.

Pitta types tend to look at relationships from a more businesslike perspective. They are concerned with the exchange; they want things to be equal. Pittas often form their relationships at work, where they spend much of their time. When a relationship changes, they are concerned with what is fair and right. They may become angry and irritated. Soothing Pittas requires cooling them off. Pittas respond visually, so they appreciate order, beauty, and waterscapes.

Kapha types take time to form meaningful relationships, but once they do, they become very attached. They don't like change, so a change in relationship is very difficult for them, and they can become depressed. Kaphas respond most strongly to taste and smell, which is why they can be emotional eaters. To help keep Kaphas' spirits up, it is best to get them exercising, socializing, and stimulated with activity.

On my Web site (www.whatsyourdosha.com), I have a free quiz to help you determine your dosha, or the dosha of someone in your life.

If you're interested in learning more about Ayurveda, you can take my eight-week e-course that is available through Daily Om (www.dailyom.com). This is great information that you can use right now to be your happiest and healthiest. And Daily Om has a "pick the price" on it, so you can choose how much you want to pay.

Notes:

Transformation Applications

- Truth. Do you always tell the truth? Look at how you say things, as well as what you say. Be honest with yourself.

- Time. What time do you give to yourself, your activities, your work, your relationships? How can you make time, or find time, to be more in balance?

- Attention. Where do you give your attention? Who do you give your attention to? How do you give your attention?

- Affection. Where do you express affection? Who do you give affection to? How do you express affection?

- Apologies. Are you one to apologize easily? Or do you hate to say, "I'm sorry"? What would make you more comfortable about apologizing?

- How can you decrease suffering today; in yourself and in others?

- How can you promote harmony in relationships today?

- How can you show someone you care about him or her today?

- What nicknames, or love codes, do you share with your loved ones?

- What's your dosha? What's your partner's dosha? What is your child's dosha? How can you use this information to maintain more harmonious relationships?

Wisdom Affirmations for Maintaining Relationships

- I am grateful for the relationships that I have, and I express this gratitude to the people in my life.
- I love the people in my life as they are, not as I want them to be or think they "should" be.
- I make myself available to the people in my life, and I know that people are available to me as well.

Chapter 5:
Changing Relationships

Let us suppose that there are two sorts of existences—
one seen, the other unseen... The seen is the changing,
and the unseen is the unchanging.

—Socrates

Seasons

Everything in life is evolving. Everything changes. We see it all around us. Plants grow, flowers bloom, then wilt, seeds are dispersed. There is a natural cycle to life. We change as people. And that's a good thing. We're not that crying baby we once were, or the toddler with tantrums. We grow physically, emotionally, mentally, and socially. We learn to get along with people, to play nice, and to share. And all the while, everyone else around us is learning and growing and changing too. So, it only makes sense that our relationships would change right along with everything else.

The only thing that never changes is spirit. And we are all connected on this level of spirit, even to people we don't know or have never met. There is an energy in the Universe that animates us, and that bring us together for specific purposes. We are here to help each other. When relationships change, and it seems like people leave us, that energy is still there. Because of this, relationships can't end. A cycle is round, not linear. There is no real beginning and no real end. We were connected before we came into this relationship, and we continue to be connected after the relationship has run its course.

Agreements

It might seem to us that we have no control over our relationships; that we just randomly meet people and some get to be our friends and some we get close to and others we just pass by for a moment. But we actually have everything to do with who we meet, and why. Spirit expresses as each one of us. In human expression, we are individual souls connected to this energy. When we are just in spirit, before we come into this lifetime, we make agreements with other souls. We decide that we're going to meet up, for some mutual benefit, and then we allow spirit to work this arrangement into the cosmic plan. Once we connect, the agreement is set into motion. We may not be aware of it, but we learn and grow as a result of it. Sometimes it is wonderful, and sometimes it is painful. But always it is something that we not only need, but that we agreed to on a very deep personal level. It takes two people to make an agreement. So in any relationship, no matter how it turns out, it is basically what we signed up for.

Since we come together to fulfill an agreement, once that agreement is fulfilled, then we can move on to fulfill other agreements. Or we can use our time and energy to learn and grow in other ways. The purpose for us being here is to learn and grow, and one very important way we do that is through our relationships. Once the agreement is fulfilled, we may perceive the relationship as being "over" or having "ended." But that's not the case at all. The agreement is complete, and, as a result, the relationship has merely changed. We have no further obligation to each other, and we can redefine the relationship however we want to.

It is important to fulfill these agreements, because if we don't we'll likely have to come back and do it all over again, until we get it right. That's the reason why so many people end up in the same type of relationships time and again. They don't "get it" the first time, so the same sort of situation arises where spirit gives them another chance at it. Some people might call this karma.

Karma

"Karma" is what we do every day—it's really another word for "action." An action (I drink a cup of coffee) creates a memory (I liked that cup of coffee), which creates a desire (I want another cup of coffee), which creates an action—and starts the cycle all over again.

To break out of our karma is like breaking our habits. We just need to do something *different*! But most of us are so conditioned that we don't even see that there is anything different to do. We need to open ourselves up to the infinite possibilities that are out there for us.

The first way to do this is by recognizing that we have a *choice*. Before automatically reaching for that cup of coffee, look at your options. Seek out your options. Research if you need to see more options. You'll be surprised. A myriad of teas, herbal teas, decaf, lattes, cappuccino, mocha, coffee substitutes, roasted barley, and so forth.

Then, choose differently, and keep choosing differently. Shake it up, go wild!

Although this is a simple example, the same thing applies to our whole lives. Did you ever wonder why you keep dating the same type of man? Instead of engaging your brain, you've gone on autopilot and fallen into habit. It's your own karma that you created. Choose differently.

Whatever it is that you want to change in your life, look at your options and choose again. You don't have to keep making the same mistake repeatedly. We are not victims of karma; we have a choice. Getting "good" karma simply means training ourselves to look at our choices, instead of robotically doing things out of habit.

How to Get "Good" Karma

Pay someone a compliment. By doing this you are raising the energy around you. You are focusing on the positive, and that is uplifting to both you and the person receiving the compliment. You are making a conscious choice here, and choosing to do something nice is good karma.

Do an anonymous good deed. This is like contributing to your karmic bank account. Don't do it for what you expect to get back; do it because you'll feel good knowing that you did it! At some point you'll be surprised when nice little things start happening to you too.

Change your routine. Shake things up a bit. Keep yourself on your toes! Too often, we sleepwalk through our day, falling back into those old habits. Just by a slight change, like parking somewhere other than the usual place, we may notice something different, which gives us a new idea that can lead to infinite possibilities.

Have a good laugh. Laughter is better than medicine—it makes you feel good without any side effects! Life is filled with joy; have you had some today? When you feel good about life, you're more likely to make choices that are good for you and your karma. One thing I love about Greg is that he makes me laugh. He can find the humorous in any situation. That is such a wonderful quality, and I certainly appreciate it. Spreading good cheer is a great way to get good karma.

Use your creativity (bake a cake). We all need to express ourselves. When we make something, it is a reflection of ourselves, our feelings. Whenever I start to feel depressed, I do something creative and it helps me to feel better right away. It gets those juices flowing, and takes me outside of myself for a while. When we make something we can share with others, we are sharing ourselves with others, and that is very good karma indeed! My friend Michele makes the most beautiful greeting cards, every one a piece of art, and each such an incredible expression of who she is and how she feels. Creativity is food for the soul. When we engage our creativity we are baking a cake and eating it, too.

Show respect to yourself and others. Recognize your own worthiness. We are each here for a purpose. We deserve to be treated with respect and reverence. Why are we so hard on ourselves and each other? We're each doing the best we can. We're here to learn and grow, and sometimes we do that by making mistakes—and that's OK.

Pay attention to what you're doing. There is a familiar phrase: "The past is history, the future is a mystery, but today is a gift, that's why it's called 'the present.'" The way to have present moment awareness, to be in the NOW, is to pay attention to what you're doing. Whether it is writing a report for work, reading to your child, or washing the dishes, give the task your complete attention. It's amazing how everything falls into place when we live moment to moment like this, instead of analyzing what's already happened or worrying about what's going to happen. Good karma comes to us effortlessly.

Communicate to connect with people. We're all in this together. There is so much that we can contribute to one another, but how do we know what that is if we don't even talk? There are no coincidences in this life! The people we meet, work with, are related to, are all there to help us on our journey—and we need to be there for them too. Reach out. Communicate and watch good karma take place right before your eyes.

Meditate. Allow the wisdom of the Universe to come to you. Set aside time and space to sit in silence. Ask questions, but don't worry about getting answers. The answers will come probably when you're not even thinking about them. Just put the questions out there, give them over, and let them go. The Universe knows of many more options than we could ever possibly be aware of. Be open to what comes your way. Look out for those "lucky" situations that show you're going in the right direction.

The Story

As relationships change and people come and go from our lives, we have to remember that we always have ourselves. We are ultimately responsible for ourselves. We can't change another person; we can only change ourselves, our behavior, and our perspective. We can only play our part and write our lines; we can't write the script for everyone involved. As things change we sometimes have to improvise. And we can't let the uncertainty of what will happen deter us. My favorite screenwriting instructor taught me: "Don't get it right, get it written." I think this applies to everything in our lives. We can't be paralyzed by fear or stuck in a sense of perfection. We just need to go ahead and do it; get out there, live our lives the best we can, and see what happens.

Movies typically have three acts. We see only those three acts, but we know there is some story that happened beforehand with the characters and that more story happens afterward. Life is kind of like that too. Each relationship has its own story that plays out. And yet, when the relationship is "over," just as when the movie is over, there is still a connection. There are still events that play out that the relationship influences in one way or another. Love, like spirit, is eternal. It lives on. It can't be destroyed.

In Act One, we establish and build our relationship. In Act Two, we maintain our relationship. Then, at the beginning of Act Three, comes some kind of a turning point, and the relationship changes. The turning point is that the soul agreement is fulfilled. It can happen in an instant, or over the course of several years. It could take us a long time to figure out what is happening.

And since there are two people in the relationship, one person could get it while the other person is left in the dark. It can be difficult to go through. We end up asking why, searching for answers, and looking desperately for some kind of meaning to it all—for closure.

Relationships change all the time. When a movie ends, the lights come up and we leave the theater. That doesn't mean we'll never see another movie. We can walk right up, buy another ticket and go into a different theater. We can do this immediately, or wait until the weekend. It's our choice. When we're in school, we take a class and we have a teacher. When the class is complete, we go on and take another class, and have another teacher. Every relationship is different, and every timeline is unique.

The mother I have today is not the mother I had growing up. Sure, there are some things about her that are the same. But when you think about how people change physically over the years, is it such a stretch to see how much people can change mentally, emotionally, and spiritually as well? We've both changed, and our relationship is completely different today than it was when I was younger. And I'm sure it will continue changing and evolving as time goes on. I would not say that my childhood was happy. My mother struggled with depression, and was even hospitalized at one point. That often took its toll on me. As the oldest child, I had much to deal with after the divorce, a lot of responsibility, and I had to grow up fast. I felt like I missed a lot of the light-heartedness that comes with just being a kid.

But I always knew my mom loved me. I remember having an allergy test. I was at the pediatrician's office—

facedown on the table, bare back scrawled like a checkerboard, each square filled with a potential allergen. It was totally miserable, itchy, painful, and uncomfortable. My mom sat with me and said, "If I could trade places with you right now, I would." I looked at her and said, "I wish you could." I remember thinking that I wouldn't trade places with anyone in my position, and that she really must love me if she would do that. But then I had my children, and I understood exactly what she meant, how she felt. Now I was a mom, and I think my mother saw me differently too.

The Catalyst

Freddy, my firstborn was a conduit for a wonderful new relationship for me with both my mother and my father. And he also drastically changed the relationship between my parents. Freddy was the very first grandchild and that baby was a miracle worker. My mom and dad had not spoken—literally, not one single word to each other—in fifteen years. Even at my wedding, and my sister's wedding, they posed for pictures but never talked to each other. My sister and I didn't push it; we were just appreciative that they could be in the same room together! When Freddy was born, my mother was staying with us, and she was a great help to me. When my dad got the news that Freddy had arrived, he jumped in the car first thing in the morning and drove all day to get to my house. I wasn't expecting him; he just showed up on my doorstep. My mom answered the door, and said, "Hi, Bill. Come on in and meet your grandson!"

What?! I felt like I just stepped into an episode of *The Twilight Zone*! My dad was beaming, full of energy. He greeted my mother with a smile, and then he made a beeline for me and Freddy. I had just finished feeding Freddy and was getting ready to see if he'd nap. He was a pretty fussy baby, up and down all the time, so I had to get in whatever spurts of sleep he would give me. My dad sat down and I handed Freddy to him. I could see my dad's heart just melt. He just stared into that little face, speechless. He was filled with love for this baby he'd just met.

I was really tired and wanted to go upstairs to rest, but was nervous about leaving my mother and father alone together downstairs. In the kitchen, I asked my mom if it was OK and she assured me she was fine, she was busy cooking. I asked my dad and he said he was happy sitting there with Freddy, and to go on up. So I did. And I said a prayer of gratitude. Since I was ten years old I had been stuck in the mire of conflict between my parents, and now it looked like they were actually getting along! I couldn't believe it.

I must have totally crashed because when I opened my eyes two hours had gone by. The house was quiet. I went downstairs and found my dad in exactly the same position I had left him in, holding Freddy, who was fast asleep. My mom was cooking up a storm and the house smelled like Thanksgiving. It was close to dinnertime, so I was a little nervous about what would happen. I gingerly approached my mother and asked if we could invite my dad to stay. She had invited him herself. That night we all ate at the same table together. Somehow,

Freddy bridged a huge gap between my parents. Now they were both grandparents. Maybe this is what it took for both of them to realize that enough time had gone by, enough growth had occurred, enough change had taken place; they could let go of resentment and finally have closure. To this day, I can't think of that meal without tearing up. It meant so much to me.

Losing a Child

Parents who have lost a child often say that the grief never ends, but that they learn to live with it. Some parents channel this grief into helping others. After his daughter, Jenna, was killed at twenty-one in a tragic bus accident in India while studying abroad, Ken Druck founded the Jenna Druck Foundation. The foundation honors Jenna's legacy as a remarkable young woman with two programs. One is Young Women's Leadership, and the other is Families Helping Families (FHF). Both bring hope and inspiration to those whose lives they touch. FHF was created to serve people in their journey through grief. Its approach is unique, focusing on recognition of and respect for the belief that grief is individual, and that there is no one way to overcome it. For more information, visit the Web site (www.JennaDruck.org).

The loss of a child before the child is born also can be devastating. We're not only grieving the loss of a child, but of the plans we had for our life with that child. Molly Roberts, M.D., M.S., is a holistic physician and codirector of LightHearted Medicine. She says that the important thing in helping a woman go through this is to follow her lead. "She will find her way through it more quickly if she is supported in her feelings, so give her the space and time to grieve the loss."

Dr. Roberts had this to say about the loss of a child by abortion: "It often isn't discussed, but mothers who elect to abort a baby can go through feelings of grief and loss as well. These are often not as easily discussed because of the circumstances, and the woman may even feel like she doesn't have a right to her feelings. Guilt and shame may linger for many years, and just opening up the discussion can be a catharsis for the woman."

It is important to feel the feelings, shed the tears, and let out the emotions rather than bottle them up. And, like Ken Druck, those who find some way to bring meaning to their loved one's death, through a charity organization or by advocating for a cause, report the most powerful healing after a loss.

Vivian Glyck wanted a second child, but she suffered miscarriages. She was distraught, until one day she realized that there were children all around the world that she could love, and mothers she could help. "Becoming a mother didn't just open my heart to my own child," she says, "but as so often happens, it opened my heart to the needs and concerns of mothers and children all around the world. I came to understand and respect mortality—that we all have a limited time to make our impact on the planet." Vivian started the Just Like My Child Foundation. Its mission is to alleviate the suffering of women, children, and families in rural Uganda by helping them to create their own long-term solutions to health care, education, and microenterprise. To read

Vivian's story and learn about her foundation, visit the Web Site (www.JustLikeMyChild.org).

Grieving

Closure is different from grieving. The *Handbook of Psychiatry* defines grief as "the normal response to the loss of a loved one by death." It also labels the response to other kinds of losses as "pathological depressive reactions." The Kübler-Ross model describes a process by which people deal with grief, loss, tragedy, or a terminal illness in five stages. These stages are now known worldwide as the Five Stages of Grief. They are:

1. **Denial.** At this stage, we don't really comprehend that we have experienced loss. We feel there must be some mistake. This can't possibly be happening.
2. **Anger.** This is the "no fair" stage. We get mad at the situation, at the person who has left, and/or at ourselves. We look to place blame. We lash out.
3. **Bargaining.** At this stage, we try to make deals with a higher power. We try to buy time, to do something—anything—that will change the situation.
4. **Depression.** At this stage, we experience deep sadness; we shut down.
5. **Acceptance.** With acceptance, we come to terms with the loss and can accept that we will be fine.

We don't always go through all of these stages, but studies show that most people go through at least two of them when dealing with loss. A loss can be any change in circumstance: an illness, a divorce, loss of freedom, someone's death, the loss of a home. When we feel a loss, it is important to grieve. Grief can be a doorway to surrender. Surrender is accepting what is. The process of grieving allows us to honor our feelings more and cry less. It is interesting that acceptance is the final stage in grieving—yet it is the second stage in achieving closure. Closure takes us beyond grieving when we need to do both. We can go through the processes simultaneously or separately. There's no one-size-fits-all approach, as every person, and every situation, is unique.

Psychoanalyst and author Alma H. Bond, Ph.D., explains why we grieve for the loss of a relationship, even when we know it is for the best. She says: "Every loss revives all the old ones. When we grieve, we mourn not just for the lost person, but for every loss from the beginning of our lives. That is why mourning takes so long, often years. Also, even the worst relationships have their good moments. We grieve for what was good and is gone forever." She says that we need to go through the process and find closure when a relationship changes, so that we can move on to new relationships. "We only have a certain amount of libido to invest in others. When it remains all tied up with a departed person, it isn't available for new relationships."

What Else We Need

Sometimes, there is a change and we don't consider it a loss; it's just a change. Or we can reframe our mind to see it as a change instead of a loss. There is no failure in life, only lessons learned. But sometimes we're done grieving, and we still can't figure out why we feel bad. Those are times we need closure. We want to understand. We want to know that there is some purpose in the pain. We want to get past focusing on the little details and asking ourselves what went wrong and why. Grieving is looking back; closure is about looking ahead. We want to let go and move on. This is what closure gives us.

Links in a Chain

Closure is actually the perfect word for it. It's more than neatly tying up loose ends. Think about life as a series of events and relationships, all linked together in some sort of artistic way, like a beautiful piece of jewelry. We can't wear a necklace or a bracelet if the chain is just left dangling. The jewelry maker finishes the piece by adding a clasp, one loop that sort of ties together the beginning and the end, the start and the finish, so that what we are left with is one strong continuous chain. Our closure is that clasp. Closure helps it all make sense. It turns something seemingly broken into something useful, purposeful, and lovely.

Closure can't come from any other party. We can't look to "get" closure from another person. We can only find closure within ourselves. It is a process we must go through on our own. As much as we would like an apology, or an explanation, or something from the other person or people involved, that doesn't always happen. And even if it does, it's not guaranteed to give us closure.

About a year after my divorce I was feeling a little unsettled, like I still needed some closure. I called Jeff and asked to see him. He was suspicious and hesitant. Maybe he thought I was going to yell at him or something—but I convinced him that everything was fine, I just wanted to talk. The truth is, I think I really wanted to feel better about things. I was feeling hurt, used, and taken advantage of, and I wanted him to apologize. I felt he owed me an apology for lying to me, hiding assets, and misrepresenting himself all those years. We did talk, but there was no way I was getting that apology—or any admission of guilt—in any way, shape, or form. But he did say something that helped me to better understand that our agreement really was fulfilled, and that I had to find my own closure. He said that while going through boxes, he found a blank book that I had filled for him. Over the years I put cartoons, drawings, poems, little memories, and photos in it for him. It was really one long love letter. He said that when he went through it, he realized that I had really loved him. And that he had never really loved me like that.

I think I knew it all along, and that's why I felt so empty much of the time during the marriage. Jeff was good at giving presents. I think that was his way of showing love. I remember feeling distance between us, and I couldn't explain it, because I really thought he loved me. I used to say to him, "Bring me a present, please!" What I was really saying, what I really meant, was, "*Be* present with me, love me." What my heart ached for more than anything was love. The gifts weren't any kind of a substitute.

For a while I tried buying myself gifts to feel better, but of course that didn't work. What I learned is that "things" do not make you who you are. A bigger diamond doesn't make you a happier person. A more expensive car does not make you a more powerful person. A job doesn't make you who you are either. Having the luxury of staying home with the kids doesn't make a person a great parent. Being the president of a company doesn't make you a good leader. And whatever someone thinks of you, good or bad, is just an opinion—it is not who you are. We need to know ourselves, and love ourselves, as the whole, perfect, complete, spiritual expression that we truly are. We can't let anything, or anyone, define us.

The Reasons Why

There are many reasons why a relationship changes. Certainly if someone dies, death is going to change your relationship. That person is not physically present for you. That doesn't mean that your relationship is over. Your memories continue. The lessons you learned from that person are a part of who you are. You will still think about that person, and likely even dream about that person. The physical body is no longer a part of this life, but the relationship is still there; it has merely changed shape. We may go through all the stages of grieving and still not feel right about it. We can't call the person back in to give us that higher perspective and some sort of an explanation. We're left here to figure it out for ourselves, which can be frustrating.

Psychologist Randy E. Kamen-Gredinger, Ed.D., says: "Relationships form the core of our sense of self and sense of connectedness. When a relationship changes either through death, divorce, moving away, illness—the experience of loss can be profound. This type of loss takes a toll on the individual physically and psychologically. It is not unusual for someone experiencing the loss of a loved one to become more likely to succumb to diseases, illnesses, and accidents. This has been shown repeatedly in the literature. Also, people experiencing the loss of an important relationship can become depressed, anxious, and can encounter a wide range of emotions." She recommends tapping into other meaningful relationships—with friends, family, therapists, or clergy—to help cope with any pain and suffering.

It is also a good idea to connect with others who have experienced something similar and share stories. Other helpful techniques include deep breathing and meditation.

Ripple Effect

In a divorce, even as spiritual and as amicable as it may be, there is still some pain, some feeling of failure. There are so many people affected by a divorce besides the actual couple. There are the in-laws, the children, the friends, the neighbors, even the pets. Any of them may seek closure from the change in the relationship too. One of the reasons I stayed so long in my first marriage was because of my relationships with the rest of the family. I didn't want to hurt anyone. I didn't want to divorce the whole family, just that one person. I knew there would be repercussions felt a long way out, and there were.

As difficult as it was for me to find closure with my marriage relationship, I also had to find closure with how my relationships had changed with the rest of the family. I tried to continue a close, warm, loving relationship with Jeff's family, but that's not what they wanted. I had been best friends with my sister-in-law. We were both pregnant at the same time, and I was godmother to two of her children. We shared many vacations together, and could really understand what the other was going through since we were married to brothers. It took us a long time to build our friendship, but once we did it was solid. Not having this close friend in my life in the same way was very hard on me. We still remain friendly when we run into each other at graduations and things like that, where the kids are involved, but it's not the same. It could have been different, but I think that Jeff's brother's point of view was that he would have been disloyal to his brother had he or his wife continued to be close to me. The same is likely true for Jeff's father, who I used to call "Dad." The three men are very tight; they lived together since the boys were teens and they grew a successful business together from the ground up. I went through all the stages of closure and have finally come to terms with the change in my relationships with these people who were once my family.

Since Jeff's mother and father were divorced long before we were married, and his mother lives in another city, my relationship with my mother-in-law did not change that much after my divorce. I think she understood what I was going through, since she went through something very similar. We have never been very close, but there has always been a mutual respect and love, and that continues. I appreciate that she has always been kind and genuine with me.

My mother was totally distraught when she learned of our plans for divorce. Jeff was a son to her; she'd watched both of us grow up and start a life together. She always saw him as the perfect guy, and he adored her too. She reached out to him and had him over for dinner a few times. I was a little uncomfortable with this, but knowing that I wanted everyone involved to feel good about our changing relationship, I let everybody do what he or she needed to do to get through it.

All of our relationships are so intertwined in this life, no matter who we are or where we go. While some of our friends were supportive about the divorce, others felt a need to take sides and choose one or the other of us. And, of course, our kids had to find closure, to figure out how the dynamics of the family were going to change.

Growing and Growing Up

As kids grow, our relationship with them changes and grows. At first, they are so dependent on us, expecting every coo and cry to be answered immediately. Then, before we know it, they're pushing us away, striving for independence. For a time they're looking over their shoulder, making sure we're still watching as they stride off on their own. But before long, they're actually screeching out of the driveway, celebrating their new-found freedom. At each of these ages we may need to find closure, as our role is redefined and our relationship adjusted.

There are significant milestones in our children's lives where the parental relationship naturally changes. When children go off to school for the first time. When they learn to drive. When they start dating. When they move away to college, or get their first apartment. When they get married. When they have children of their own. We see the outward manifestation of the change, and how it is impacting the child. We also need to look at how the change is affecting us, and how we are handling it, to adjust the relationship and function with the change.

Brian recently graduated from high school, and for his senior yearbook tribute ad, I included the same quote that opened this chapter, and wrote this note to him:

> *Let us suppose that there are two sorts of existences—one seen, the other unseen… The seen is the changing, and the unseen is the unchanging.*
>
> *—Socrates*
>
> *We have seen you change and grow so much over the years. And yet your heart, your sweet spirit, has not changed at all. You have become more of who you really are. You have grown into yourself, and brought forth your skills and talents. We are so proud of you, and we love you so much.*
>
> *—Dad, Mom, Greg, and Freddy*

Now that Brian is away at college, I miss having him around. The house seems very quiet without him here every day. But we talk on the phone, and e-mail, and he comes to visit quite often. Our relationship has changed, and in some ways we're closer than ever, because I don't have to play the role of the nagging parent, asking him to do laundry or make his bed. Our conversations have gotten deeper and more meaningful as Brian has matured and learned about the world. We have more to share with each other.

And as we age, the relationship that we have with life changes. We may change careers, or have to give up a favorite sport, deal with physical limitations, or retire. We face challenges where having closure helps to get us through to the next one.

We have friends come and go from our lives. Our roommates move out, get married, or move away. Our coworkers leave for another job, or retire. Or we may have a falling out, one of us hurts the other and the relationship can't be repaired. These "friendship divorces" can be just as painful as a regular divorce, and we need closure just as much.

Whatever the situation, closure can help give us peace of mind. It can help us to move forward with our lives, without regret. In the following chapters we will discuss the five stages of closure and how we can apply them to any of our changing relationships, so that we can handle things with grace and clear intention. The stages are:

1.**Recognition**
2.**Acceptance**
3.**Understanding**
4.**Integration**
5.**Gratitude**

Notes:

Transformation Applications

- Look at the agreements that you have entered into with the different relationships you have. Are they clear? Are they ongoing? When will your agreement be fulfilled? How will your relationship change when the agreement is fulfilled?
- What lessons have you learned from the different people in your life? Who have been your teachers in your life? Are there relationships you would like to pursue that could help bring wisdom to you?
- How has karma shown up in your life? What actions can you take to see the results you want to see in your life?
- When and where have you experienced grief in your life? How did you move through it? Are you still moving through it? Have you gone through each of the stages of grief?
- How have relationships changed in your life over the years?

Wisdom Affirmations for Changing Relationships

- I know that the world is constantly evolving and that the people in it are too.
- I know that change is inevitable and can bring about new relationships.
- Change is a conduit for learning and growth, and I look for how I can learn and grow with this experience.

Part 2

The Five Stages
of Closure

Chapter 6:
Recognition

No one remains quite what he was when he recognizes himself.

—Thomas Mann

The first stage in the five stages of closure is Recognition. We must first recognize that the relationship has changed, or is changing. We get complacent in our relationships, and we often expect them to just go along on autopilot. While we are busy paying attention to something else, big changes may be occurring that we're not even aware of. It took me a long time to recognize that my marriage was ending, that my relationship with Jeff had changed. I didn't want to see it, I had too many other things to deal with, and I always felt that the commitment would get us through whatever conflicts came up. I really didn't consider that I had any other choice but to stay married. We first started seeing a marriage counselor after about our eight-year anniversary. We went on and off for the next nine years. Things would get better, and then go back to how they had been.

Read the Signs

What I needed to see was that we both weren't happy. Jeff would tell me straight out, "I'm not happy." But I didn't consider that divorce would make a difference.

He'd put me down, really trying to push me away. All the signs were there, but I wouldn't read them. I don't know if I didn't want to or if I was so distracted with everything else that I couldn't handle one more thing. There finally came a time when I needed to recognize that the relationship had changed so much over the years, little by little, that it was not the marriage that either of us wanted anymore. Our agreement, whatever it was, was fulfilled, and we weren't doing each other any good staying together. Once the recognition was there, on both our parts, then the stagnation ended. The door opened, the light came in, and we started looking at all the choices we had.

When a relationship changes, the energy shifts. It just feels different from how it felt before. You might not be able to put your finger on it, but you can definitely sense that the change is there. It doesn't matter how the change is initiated, or why; the dynamics of the relationship are not the same. It can be subtle, occurring over a long period of time, or it can be sudden and abrupt. When we are tuned in we can feel it. It doesn't necessarily mean something is wrong, just that something is different.

Our first instinct, when something like this happens, is to look at the other person. We look at what the person is doing, analyze his or her every move, and try to figure out the person's motives. We take things personally. "Why did he or she do this to me?" That is exactly what we should NOT be doing! Don Miguel Ruiz says, in his book *The Four Agreements:* "Don't Take Anything Personally." We can't control another person, or his or her behavior. But we have control over our own behavior. When it comes to your life, you are both the screenwriter and the star. Remember that you are not a victim. You have played your part in this scenario, and now you've come to the end of the script. Recognize your role, and recognize that you are now free to play new roles, starting immediately. Now is the time to look at yourself. Look at what you are doing. Look at how you are acting, and reacting. No blaming, no complaining. Decide how you can best handle things. Be true to yourself; be genuine and authentic, with integrity and dignity. Be aware of your words and actions. Personalize this quote for yourself; from Swami Prajnananpad: "Live your own life. That is to say, where you are, with what you are, and with who you are."

Yes, that particular relationship has changed. Now look at what has not changed. You are still here. Recognize that the "unseen" is the unchanged. The love that was created is still here, and on some level it always will be. Spirit is still here. Wisdom is still here. Choices are still here. Right here, right now.

Breaking Up

Dr. Molly Roberts says that when ending a relationship that is no longer working, it is best to be compassionate with yourself and your partner as you make the changes you need to make. "The first step is to recognize that this relationship was a dance, and that you both were contributing members for the good times and the bad. This will help you to resist the urge to demonize your partner or to take all the blame." When on the receiving end of such news, the same advice applies. "All this means is that this one person isn't the right match for you. It says nothing about your own worth. At the same time, it is important to say that your previous partner doesn't owe you their life or their love. We all have a right to decide who we want to be intimate with, and if they have made a decision to leave the relationship, it is important that you give them the same respect you would want for yourself. This is a time to gather your dignity and grace, not to squander it."

Unexpected Change

Sometimes the change comes harshly. That's how it was when I found out that my friend Ophir had died. I remember getting a phone call from our mutual friend Curt. He was in disbelief and distraught, as he had just gotten the news. It took a few phone calls to figure out exactly what had happened. Ophir had committed suicide.

I knew Ophir as an extremely talented and creative composer. We worked together on several music projects. We had a close friendship and a great respect for each other. Ophir helped me bring my songs to life. When Ophir had a hernia operation, I had him stay at my home while he recovered.

I was aware that Ophir used drugs. I spoke with him about it many times, offering him alternatives and suggestions for a more healthy way of life. But he did not want to hear it. He did not want to talk about it. He always functioned perfectly well when we were working, and he assured me that he did not have a problem. When I heard that Ophir had died, I assumed it was an accidental overdose. But there was no accident about Ophir's death. He planned it. He put a rifle in his mouth and shot himself.

Unanswered Questions

Like most people in this situation, I started asking myself all kinds of questions. What could I have done to prevent this? Why didn't I see this coming? What was so terrible that he had to do this? I felt awful, not only for myself, but for his family and everyone who loved him. Suicide is such a violent act. It is terribly hurtful to all those left behind with so many unanswerable questions. I don't know what brought Ophir to his decision. I do know and recognize that although our relationship has changed, he is still very much a part of my life. I have the songs we wrote together on my Web sites. He taught me so much about music and the creative process. When certain songs are played on the radio, I am reminded of him, and his amazing energy, sweet smile, and sly sense of humor. His words still influence me. His music still moves me.

I know the agreement that Ophir and I had was complete even before his death. There was no unfinished business between us. We learned from each other, both creatively and personally. At his funeral I met many others who felt the same way.

This was the second time I had been affected by suicide. When I was around eleven years old, shortly after my parents' divorce, my mother's brother took his life. He was a Vietnam veteran, and he became hooked on drugs while in the war. When he got home, he couldn't handle normal life after everything he saw in combat. His drug problem got worse, he would have hallucinations, and he overdosed to escape the pain.

I saw how this shattered my mother and grandmother. He also left behind a wife and a baby daughter. It was tragic. As a child, I could sense how awful this was for everyone. And now, as an adult, I can see how my uncle's life mattered. Even in the short time he was with us, he brought joy to his mother and love to his family. He struggled with life, and he chose to die. But while he was here he lived, and he had the opportunities and experiences that allowed him to learn and grow. He may not have made the best choices, but they were his choices. In situations like this, you have to get past the blame, and the guilt, and know that there is nothing you could have done to change the outcome. For whatever reason, this person took his own life. It is not rational, or logical, or right. But it is irreversible. And we learned by going through all of this together as a family.

Chaim Nissel, Psy.D., is the director of Yeshiva University's Counseling Center in New York City, and an expert with the American Association of Suicidology. He has this to say about coping with the loss of a loved one from suicide:

The death of a loved one by suicide has all the trappings of conventional grief plus a host of other intense, difficult and confusing emotions. These include feelings of guilt and responsibility, anger and blame and often a disconnect with the individual who killed himself. When we lose a loved one to cancer or AIDS, we accept the reality, feel the loss, grieve, yet we don't blame ourselves. Following a suicide, it is hard to accept the reality that the individual chose death. We feel responsible and wonder "if I had only..." he'd be alive today. We would rather blame ourselves because it is difficult to place the responsibility where it belongs, on the individual who killed himself.

One who experiences the death of a loved one to suicide is fittingly called a "survivor." They must now learn to cope and survive their loss. Most survivors experience anger, guilt and emotional turmoil. There is often anger at the deceased for taking their own life, it is seen as selfish, because their pain ends, but the survivor's pain begins. Guilt over what they could have and should have done to prevent it (although if the loved one wanted to die, they would have despite your interventions). We like to think that we can control events, but when another person is in such emotional pain that they want to die, the choice to kill themselves remains their choice, despite everything that you can and did offer them.

There is still tremendous stigma and shame associated with suicide and when the fact that one died by suicide is hidden or denied, it becomes so much more difficult to come to terms with it. When we try to "cover" or pretend the death was accidental, it takes its toll on the survivors and will impact them the rest of their lives.

To help us find closure, Dr. Nissel has this advice:

- Talk about it. Find supportive people in your life that you can share your feelings with.
- Focus on the person's life, and the good memories you have of the person. Know that you will never truly know why he killed himself.
- Recognize that the person's pain is over, and now it's time to start healing your own pain.
- Have answers prepared for when people ask questions. This will help reduce your anxiety and emotional reactions. You can say, "He took his own life," or "He died by suicide," or even "He suffered a long illness." If someone is persistent, blaming, or insensitive, you can say, "It is too difficult to talk about right now," and end the conversation.
- Know that you are not responsible for your loved one's death, in any way. Only the individual who killed him or herself is responsible.
- Know that the likelihood is that the person was in such pain, for so long, and now the suffering is over. Ninety percent of those that die by suicide suffered from some form of mental illness, most commonly an affective disorder such as depression or bipolar disorder.
- Seek resources such as professional counseling, support groups, and books.
- Being exposed to a suicide makes you somewhat more susceptible to suicidal thinking. If you are having thoughts of killing yourself, get help

immediately by contacting a psychologist or psychiatrist. If you feel you may act on these suicidal impulses, call 911 or go to your local emergency room.

Community

Unfortunately, suicide is common. It is the second-leading cause of death in college students. The American Foundation for Suicide Prevention (afsp.org) helps survivors of suicide. It has a National Survivors of Suicide Day in November. Actress Michelle Ray Smith, who played Ava on the daytime drama *Guiding Light,* talked about her father's suicide in an interview with *Soap Opera Digest* magazine. She said that participating in AFSP's "Out of the Darkness" event, an overnight twenty-mile walk, helped her connect with people who had been through the same thing. "For the first time since he died—it's been three years in September—I feel at peace." Talking with people, sharing our stories, is one way that we can help each other to heal.

To help us recognize what has changed, and what has not changed, in our lives when something like this happens, it is good to reach out to our community. There are many groups we can connect with; we don't have to feel so isolated. I read in our local paper about a woman named Michele Neff Hernandez who lost her husband in a bicycle accident. She scoured the Internet for resources and didn't find what she needed, so she started a Web site of her own (WidowsBond.com). It is a place where widows can connect. "It can be an avenue for talking about things other people don't understand, airing feelings that are overwhelming, and finding comfort in knowing you are not alone," she said. SoldiersAngels.org is a Web site started by the mother of a soldier serving in the current war. CafeMom.com is a social networking site where moms can connect and talk about various issues they are facing with their children.

And of course, there are local groups, too. Parents Without Partners has been around for many years; my mother joined when she got divorced. When I found out that Freddy had attention deficit disorder, I joined our local chapter of Children and Adults with Attention Deficit Disorders (CHADD; chadd.org) to connect with other parents and share experiences and resources. I don't know how I would have gotten through that very difficult and confusing time in my life without the help of the new friends I made there. We relied on each other because we totally understood what we were all going through, and there was no judgment, only support. We can help each other recognize our own strength, and recognize that although the relationship has changed, all of the really important stuff, like love, will never change.

Seven Months

My friend Tammy's mother died at a young age, and Tammy always thought that she would die young too. Tammy had been feeling very sick and just wasn't getting better, so she decided to see her doctor, who ran a battery of tests. He asked Tammy to meet him in his office for the results. Tammy just knew it was going to be bad news. She thought about how she was going to put her affairs in order, how she was going to tell her husband. She sat down and solemnly asked the doctor, "How much time do I have?" The doctor said, "I'd say you have seven months." Tammy broke down and cried. It seemed way too soon. The doctor looked perplexed. "I thought you would be happy!" he said. "Happy? Why would I be happy that I'm dying?" Tammy sobbed. The doctor smiled. "You're not dying. You're pregnant. You're going to have a baby in seven months!"

Needless to say, this news changed Tammy's life, and her relationships, dramatically. She now recognized that she was not her mother, and that she indeed had a very full life to lead. It opened up her heart to a new love and a new purpose.

When we're kids and we grow it's easy to recognize the changes. We outgrow our clothes. Our shoes don't fit and we need new ones. But when we grow on the inside, sometimes it is not as easy to recognize at first. And yet, the outward expression of it can be just as obvious. We outgrow a job and get a promotion, or start a new business. We outgrow our old value system and shed the relationships that don't serve us or support a healthy and happy lifestyle. We need to open our eyes to recognize that our relationships are changing as the first step to bring ourselves closure.

Still, many of us don't want to recognize change. We fear it, so we avoid it and look away. We use stall tactics, and keep putting on those too-tight shoes. We're only hurting ourselves! We are postponing the inevitable. How often have you heard: "I'll be happy when _____"—fill in the blank—I get that new job, I have my bills paid off, I am in a committed relationship, I have a baby, the kids finish school, and so on, ad infinitum! There is no time like the present. If you can't be happy now, exactly as things are, what is the point? NOW is the only time that exists; there is no later, because later turns into now. *A Course in Miracles* says: "This instant is the only time there is." You have the power, you have the control, and you have the choice, this very instant. See it and do something about it.

Change can be tragic and painful, but we can and do get through it. Change can also be disruptive. It can shake us up and cause us to grow and expand in ways we never thought possible. And change can be absolutely wonderful. It can bring to us new experiences and opportunities, introduce us to new people, and bring more love into our lives. And it can be all these things at the same time. The first step to recognize change, and to recognize that there is much more to this change than we can see at the moment. More information will unfold for us as time goes on and we see what happens.

Notes:

Transformation Applications

- Note the changes in your relationships from the past. Do you remember:

    Your first friend?

    Your first date?

    Your first kiss?

    Your first teacher?

    Your first crush?

- Observe the person you were then, and see the changes in the person you are now.

- Look at how endings can become beginnings. Where has this been true in your life?

- Take stock of your relationships from the past. Rather than look at what you've lost from those relationships being changed, look at what you gained that you still carry with you. Don't look at what you don't have; instead, look at what you do have.

Wisdom Affirmations for Recognition

- I recognize that although external factors may change, the eternal factors remain constant.
- I know that change takes place in time and space, and that as time goes on, change becomes easier.
- I look at my feelings about this shift, and how the change is affecting me, mentally, physically, and emotionally.

Chapter 7:
Acceptance

The secret of solitude is that there is no solitude.
—Joseph Cook

The second stage in closure is Acceptance. Acceptance means not only do you recognize that the change in relationship is taking place, but also that you are OK with it. You may not understand why this is happening, but you know that somehow, at some point, everything is going to be just fine. It is knowing that even though it might not feel great right now, it won't always be this way.

A Change of Plans

I pretty much had my life all planned out. I married young, had Freddy at our three-year anniversary point, and got pregnant with baby number two so that the kids would be two years apart. But life had other plans for me. I lost the baby in my first trimester. I was devastated. It had taken a while for me to get pregnant, and I really wanted this child. I was very invested in giving Freddy a sibling. I definitely felt a loss, an emptiness. My doctor assured me that I would get pregnant again, but that we would have to wait awhile to try so that my body could heal. Fortunately, Brian came along fairly soon after that.

After two kids, I was done. Pregnancy was not fun for me at all. I was sick every day, I couldn't work, I couldn't sleep, and my feet swelled so much I could hardly find shoes to wear. Plus, I had my hands full with two kids, and I felt a strong social responsibility to reproduce only two people to replace the two parents who would leave the earth at some point. Jeff wanted more kids, but since it takes two people to make this important decision, we practiced birth control.

Imagine my surprise when I found myself pregnant yet again. I cried. This was not what I wanted, and I felt terrible for not wanting it. Jeff was elated. It took me a long time to accept the pregnancy, and to be happy about it. I came to the conclusion that this is what was meant to be, so I was going to go along with it and celebrate it. I had an ultrasound and my doctor assured me that everything looked great. Jeff told his family. His dad came over and brought flowers, which was very unlike him—he rarely visited because he saw his sons at work every day.

But then I started bleeding, much as I had done the first time I miscarried. I was really worried, and started to be super-careful about everything I did. I felt that I had already bonded with this baby and I didn't want to lose it. But a few days later, that's exactly what happened. It was a nightmare for me. I felt empty and emotionally drained. First, I had to recognize and accept that I had a relationship with this unborn child. Then, I had to recognize and accept that our relationship had changed; that this child was not going to be born after all. I had to accept that there was an agreement between the two of us, that the baby needed to experience this time with me for some reason, and that I needed to have this experience. I did my part and the baby did its part. And now the agreement was fulfilled. Of course, I still had to go through the other subsequent stages to get closure about it.

Forgive, Detach, Let Go

Acceptance comes when we release blame, when we release resentment. Acceptance comes when we forgive. When we forgive, we give a gift of peace to ourselves. By not forgiving, we continue to experience pain. We're only hurting ourselves. It is self-abuse. There is a saying that not forgiving is like drinking poison and expecting the other person to die. It doesn't work.

Acceptance comes when we can detach from the circumstances. When we can look at life as a movie, when we can stand back and watch our scenes play out, then we get the kind of perspective it takes to accept things as they are, not as we would wish them to be.

Acceptance means that we can let go. There is freedom in simplicity. Whether we're talking about toxic emotions, or clutter, or excess weight, it's all just "stuff." My friend Sherry said that once she made peace with her ex-husband, once she accepted the change in their relationship and quit blaming him, she lost nineteen pounds. She felt lighter in body, mind, and spirit. She realized she needed to stop carrying around the hurt; that it was literally weighing her down. And she was right! She is so much happier now, and she looks and feels absolutely terrific. It was a decision—a decision to let go.

Let go of grievances. *A Course in Miracles* says: "Love holds no grievances." The core concept in *A Course in Miracles* is that there is only love or fear. All through life we must choose between these two things. This is what we see, love, or fear. This is what we feel, love, or fear. And when it all boils down to it, what is fear? Just as darkness is a lack of light, fear is a lack of love. So there is only love. Choose love. Accept love. Love is all there is.

"Stuff"

Our "stuff" carries a lot of energy with it. Just like my old house had the memories in the walls, our clothes, our furniture, it all picks up on the energy around it. Old, negative energy which doesn't serve us anymore needs to be moved out. Get rid of broken-down items, they are representative of the things in your life that you perceive as broken down. You don't need to be carrying it around, literally or figuratively. Lighten up! Whatever you haven't used, or worn, in a year, give to charity. Let someone who really needs it and appreciates it have it. Let it go. It brings greater clarity when things are organized and in order. I had some rings that Jeff had given me that I really didn't want to wear anymore because I felt like they represented my "old" life, and I was ready to start anew. So rather than give them away, I took them in to a jewelry store and had the stones set into a necklace. It's totally different and I love it.

I also didn't feel the need to have as much stuff around. Some of the collections I had that were just gathering dust or taking up cupboard space I sold on eBay. I spent the money fixing up things in our new house.

My friend Sandy has been divorced for two years now, and yet she still feels stuck. She sees that her former husband has moved on and it bothers her. "And it bothers me that it bothers me!" she said to me over lunch one day. She was desperately seeking closure, but was having a hard time getting past the acceptance part. We talked, and Sandy explained that her ex had moved out and gotten a new house, and she was still in the same place, literally and figuratively. "It's easy for him to move forward when he's left all his baggage with me," she said, exasperated. Her house represented a lot of her marriage. There were things that he bought and she never liked. There were things that were falling apart that he never got around to fixing. The whole space was a reminder to her of all that went wrong. She wasn't in a position to move, so instead I suggested she do a big purging. Out with the junk! She moved some furniture around, got a handyman in, and took a few carloads to the Salvation Army. You can feel the difference now when you walk in the door, and Sandy feels so much better too.

When Greg and I moved to our new home, I decorated in a different style and colors than I had in my old place. I wanted a whole new energy. I loved our comfy couch, so I had it recovered in new fabric. Anything you can do to make your place feel fresh and clean will help you to detach, move on, and accept the change in relationship. A fresh coat of paint, especially in a cheery new color, does wonders for a room!

If there have been arguments in a home, or any negativity, the energy can be cleared with sage. It's a Native American ritual and it is very effective. You can buy sticks of dried sage that are bundled together. You light the sage, and then blow out the fire so that the sticks are still burning, but just with smoke, no flame. Open all the windows and walk through the house counterclockwise waving the sage around so that the smoke gets into every corner. All of the negative energy goes right out the windows! While you're doing this, sing a happy song, or say happy words like joy, peace, and love. Know that good, positive energy will come in to fill in the spaces. When you're done, say a prayer of gratitude and close the windows.

Another way you can prevent negative energy from entering the home is to sprinkle sea salt around the whole house. Start outside, at the front door, and work your way around counterclockwise until you're back at the front door again. Negative energy won't cross this protective barrier.

Makeover

Freshening up yourself can do wonders too! On soap operas, when the leading lady gets a new boyfriend, she often gets a new hairstyle. That's one way the writers show that she has evolved into this new relationship. Even a new lipstick, or a new necktie, will get you thinking more in the present moment than in the past.

My neighbor Linda is a single mother. She has two boys, one in college and one in high school. The younger son, who lives with her, has a variety of issues, so she constantly has her hands full with him. Her mother passed away years ago, and her husband died while they were in the middle of their divorce. Soon after she moved into this house, her father was ailing, so she moved him in with her so that she could take care of him.

I had met Linda only once, a few months back, right after she moved in, so I didn't know all of this was going on in her life when I called her to get a signature for some work we were doing in our backyard. Our homeowners' association requires that we fill out a form and get the neighbors to sign it before they'll approve anything. Linda finally called me back one night around ten thirty and said she was home if I wanted to come over. So I did.

When I got there, a nurse answered the door. Linda's father was in a hospital bed in her spare bedroom, on hospice care. Linda brought me into her family room and asked about the form, which now felt like such a trivial detail. We got that out of the way and I asked how she was doing. She told me everything. My heart went out to her for all she was going through. Her troubled sixteen-year-old son was in crisis care and she had just seventy-two hours to figure out what to do next. Over the years they had seen various specialists, and he was still having major issues. She had no idea where to turn, and felt overwhelmed that all of this was going on at the same time as her father was dying.

I told her about my experiences with Freddy and gave her some resources. As a mother, I could relate to what she was going through. We were instantly friends. When I got home, I made a list of numbers for her to call and left it on her door the next morning. All in the same weekend, Linda's father passed away and her son was escorted to a treatment facility in another state. Two of the most important relationships in her life had changed dramatically.

A few days later I went over to check on Linda. She greeted me with a big hug. She was so grateful for the information I had given her. I was very grateful to have a new friend. She filled me in on everything that had happened. I was quite taken with her resilience. She had a great deal to process and was handling it all very gracefully. But she looked worn-out. All that she had been through really showed on her face and in her body language. I could tell she wasn't taking care of herself—she didn't have the time or the energy to do anything but go through the motions of planning a funeral and try to save her son from a potential crisis.

The Universe orchestrates to support our desires. We just need to pay attention. There are no coincidences. Everything happens for a reason. The next day, I got an e-mail from one of my subscribers and a myspace friend, Angelique, who works at Billy Yamaguchi's salon at the Four Seasons Hotel in Westlake Village, right by my house. Billy Yamaguchi is a stylist to the stars, and he is famous for his "Feng Shui Beauty" makeovers. This sounded intriguing to me, something that would fit in well with the vision of my Internet TV show, *CoffeyTalk: Ancient Wisdom, Modern Style*. We talked about it and decided to set up a shoot for later in the month. Angelique asked if she should get a model for the shoot, or if I had a friend who would be up for a makeover. Ah!

Perfect timing. I told her I was pretty sure I could find someone.

I called Linda and made the offer. Would she be interested in a day at this beautiful salon, new hair color, style, and makeup? She sounded nervous. "You mean, in front of people?" she asked. "Not exactly in front of people," I tried to explain, "in front of a camera." She laughed, took a deep breath, and agreed.

The Yamaguchi Salon is exquisite. Serene, with a definite sense of style. Billy is warm and engaging. Linda felt comfortable with him right away, and allowed herself to be immersed in the experience. What I love about Billy's Feng Shui makeovers is that his philosophy is all about bringing out the best in the person. It's about letting that inner beauty show on the outside. It doesn't have anything to do with the latest trends; it has to do with what makes you look and feel your best. From the questionnaire and a little conversation, and also considering face shape and lifestyle, Linda and Billy determined that what she needed to do was enhance her fire element. Billy was so gracious, and we all had a lot of fun.

The day flew by. Linda got her hair cut and colored, and then Angelique did her makeup. I don't think the smile left Linda's face all day. It wasn't just the new look, it was also the whole process of paying attention to herself for the first time in a long while. She felt pampered, she felt refreshed, she felt that this day represented a whole new beginning for her. And it did. When we looked at the before and after photos, the difference was astounding. Not just in Linda's appearance, because she is a beautiful woman, but also in her demeanor, her attitude, the way she carried herself. It was remarkable. It was just what she needed. She hugged Billy with such gratitude.

To continue with the process, I helped Linda to Feng Shui her house. We added elements of fire to liven things up; bright bold colors brought much-needed energy to her monochromatic living room. We brought in some beautiful flower arrangements and hung a colorful fan over her fireplace. She had a collection of Asian figurines from her mother, and I noticed that among them were the emperor and the empress, symbols of love and marriage. I had Linda put these figures in a place of prominence in the room, so that they would be more noticeable.

Shortly after the transformation, Linda went to the car dealership to trade in her old car for a new one. Her lease was up, so the timing was perfect. Turns out, she hit it off with the salesman. So, not only did she get a new car, she also got a new boyfriend!

Forest and Trees

When my friend Scott was about eighteen years old he got hit in the head with a baseball. In the emergency room, they took an X-ray of his skull. Rather than a broken bone, what they found was a brain tumor, one that had been there for quite some time. That incident led to the first of many surgeries that Scott would go through over the years, to have tumors removed from his brain.

Scott's future was always uncertain. He loved nature and loved being outdoors. He worked taking care of the trees in the city, and spent as much time as he could hiking, skiing, mountain climbing, and hunting for his favorite wild mushrooms. He embraced life and all that it had to offer. At the same time, he was in and out of the hospital, trying various treatments, therapies, and medications. There was something so calm and wonderful about Scott. He never showed any fear. He was full of love for his family and his friends.

At some point, Scott must have known that his time was limited. He recognized that his relationships would change, and he accepted it. He drove down to visit my sister and me. He and his brother had lived across the street from us while we were growing up, and Scott and Marci had dated in high school. We all kept in touch, but didn't get much chance to see each other, living so far away. After lunch, Scott went back to Marci's house and met her husband and kids. They all rode bikes and hung out and had a great time. Although we spoke on the phone and e-mailed a few times after that day, that was the last time we saw Scott. He died at age forty.

Scott was an inspiration to so many people. He lived with this illness for all of his adult life, and yet I never heard him complain, or regret, or speak any harsh words. He was so sweet and always had a smile on his face. Because Scott was accepting and gracious, he made it easier on everyone around him to follow his example. What I learned from Scott is to see the forest and the trees, the big picture and the view right in front of my face. He was grateful for the beauty in nature, and knew what was important in life. He showed love for his family and friends, and never took one moment for granted.

Roses and Thorns

The rose flower is fragrant and sweet, and its petals are soft. And yet, we wouldn't have the beautiful flower without the stem, which is full of thorns. We can choose to focus on the thorns, and avoid the flower out of fear. Or we can enjoy the flower, knowing that the thorns are just part of the package. When we accept the rose as it is, we can benefit from it. Our changing relationships can benefit us in much the same way. We know the thorns are there—the pain we may go through or the sorrow we may feel. But we don't have to make the thorns more important than the flower—the love, lessons, memories, and experiences we shared.

Feel Fine

The lyrics of one R.E.M. song say, "It's the end of the world as we know it, and I feel fine." That's acceptance. It may be the end of the world as we know it, but it's not the end of the world. It's a change. We can adapt. We can feel fine because we really are fine.

Notes:

Transformation Applications

- How can you express yourself and your emotions? Try writing, painting, sculpting, building—anything creative where you have something to show for your efforts.

- Look at all the "stuff" in your house and on your desk. Sometimes, things have been there so long that you don't see them anymore. Ask a friend to help you look with another pair of eyes. What doesn't "fit"? What can you release? Donate? Sell? Clutter is indicative of our emotions and represents confusion. Clear the clutter and you will clear your mind.

- Look at yourself in the mirror. How do you look? Is it time for some change in your appearance? Choose a new hairstyle or outfit that better represents the present you.

Wisdom Affirmations for Acceptance

- I accept change as a part of my process of growth. I accept that growth can be painful, and I can handle it.
- I detach, so that I may move forward in positive new directions.
- I take care of myself, giving myself the time I need to be in balance.

Chapter 8:
Understanding

Those who understand only what can be explained understand very little.

—Marie von Ebner-Eschenbach

After Acceptance, the next stage to finding closure is Understanding. This can be the most difficult stage to go through, because often what we need to understand is that there are some things that are just beyond our human capacity of understanding. Yet, when we can get some kind of clarity, then we can learn and grow from the experience so that the cycle doesn't repeat. We can "get it" and move on.

And just understanding what we are going through is huge. This is another reason why it is beneficial to associate with people who have gone through similar changing relationships. They can relate and help us to make sense of things, so that we can better understand what is happening. A change in relationship is stressful, and can affect us mentally, physically, and emotionally.

Stress

Candace Pert, in her book *Molecules of Emotion*, explains scientifically how stress can create toxins that are stored in our fat cells. This stress can literally make us sick. And even worse, those cells can drive old patterns of behavior, so that we become even more stressed. We all felt the stress with the tragedy of 9/11. Even if we were miles away, our hearts were right there with all those who were suffering.

The death of someone we didn't know personally can still have a profound effect on us. John Donne in "For Whom the Bell Tolls" said: "Each man's death diminishes me, for I am involved in mankind." I remember exactly where I was and what was happening when I found out Princess Diana had died. The whole world mourned. It felt very personal to me. Diana was my age, she had two boys, as I did, and I had watched her get married. It felt as though I had lost a friend. And I know that many people felt the same way. We're all connected in spirit, so it is natural to feel sad. I felt the same way when John F. Kennedy died, and more recently, Heath Ledger, and Michael Jackson. The spontaneous tributes of flowers and candles and handwritten notes illustrate what an impact these deaths had on so many people.

Until Death Do Us Part

I met Fred when we were both working as pages at ABC-TV. We were fast friends and had so much fun together. I was dating Jeff at the time, and Fred would always say, "Introduce me to your sister!" Years later, when Marci moved down here, I had Fred take her around to look at apartments, and about a year or so later they got married. They had two kids, A. J. and Emma, two dogs, and a house—a nice family life.

One morning, Marci called me and there was an urgency in her voice. She said that Fred was sick and had been taken by ambulance to the hospital. He had collapsed on the floor and couldn't feel his legs. She was very scared. It turned out that Fred had a dissected aortic aneurism. He was flown by helicopter to another hospital and underwent emergency surgery. I went over to Marci's house to stay with the kids after school and ended up staying the night. We didn't know what was going to happen. Fred survived the surgery, but the doctor called in the middle of the night saying they needed to do another surgery on Fred's legs because he was in danger of becoming a paraplegic.

The next three weeks were intense and terrifying. We didn't know if Fred would live or die. We didn't know if he'd ever be able to walk or talk again. We were dealing with all kinds of doctors and trying to understand what was happening. So many machines and tubes, and more surgeries. It was confusing, and frustrating, and so incredibly sad. Inside this hospital day after day, it was a surreal experience; isolated from the world and looking desperately for answers. Marci and I clung to each other. We were the only ones who understood what we were going through. It was awful for everyone. Fred's mother was distraught, simply heartbroken. We did our best to comfort her. Fred's brother could hardly speak. He was devastated.

A. J. was sixteen at the time, so he drove himself and Emma to and from the hospital. He has a strong and quiet demeanor, and carries so much inside. He's not a person who is easy to get to know, but during this experience I got to really know him—and to feel his heart, which was breaking. Emma, at fourteen, was all over the place emotionally. She and I have always been close; we're a lot alike. She was having such a hard time trying to understand the "why" behind all this. At times she was inconsolable. I did my best to help her know that she was safe and loved, no matter what happened with her dad.

Fred never fully regained consciousness. After an MRI showed irreparable damage to both his brain and heart he was taken off life support. That night, Marci called all of Fred's family and friends, and we each had a chance to say good-bye to him. We shared stories and memories, remembering happier times with Fred. We stayed for a long time, since being with each other helped us feel closer to him.

As sad as we are when someone we love dies, we have to understand that all of us have our own paths. All of us have our own purposes and our own agreements to work on in this lifetime. When those agreements are fulfilled, it represents growth and is cause for celebration. And it is time to move on, in one way or another. I found this beautiful quote, and it has given me comfort in times when I get caught up in the emotions that come with losing someone close to me:

> *Nature is forever giving us chance after chance at what we call rebirth and death, and we, in our folly, in our fear of death, fail to understand that which represents a new journey, a new page on which to write, and thus to believe in a new beginning for ourselves.*
> —*Shri Parthasarathi Rajagopalachari*

We'll never understand exactly what happened, or why. It's beyond comprehension. We just have to trust that whatever Fred set out to do in this lifetime, he did.

His agreements were fulfilled. And we can understand what we went through during those three weeks, and allow ourselves to heal from that.

Stress Assessment

There is a test, based on the work of mental health experts Thomas H. Holmes and Richard H. Rahe, which can help us identify the sources and amount of stress that we encounter in life. The test consists of a list of forty-three stress-inducing events, ranked in order of their "Life Change Unit" from high to low. The idea is to look at the life events that a person has encountered during a given year, add up the units, and use the score to determine the degree of stress we're under, and our chances for accidents or illnesses because of it. Of the forty-three events, twenty of them directly have to do with some change in relationship. The top three events are: death of a spouse, divorce, and marital separation. Two events are tied for fourth: death of a close family member and serving a jail term. Clearly, a change in a relationship is a stressful event in our lives, and if we have more than one in any given year, it can take its toll on us. It helps to understand what we are going through so that we can implement stress-reducing techniques into our lifestyle.

PTSD

The death of a loved one or a divorce can be traumatic. And many of us end up suffering from post traumatic stress disorder (PTSD) without even knowing it. It can happen months, or even years after the fact.

Trauma can also be a cause of soul fragmentation. This is a condition where we dissociate from reality as a coping mechanism to avoid feeling the emotional pain. We can experience this as depression, anxiety, apathy, or even addiction.

Three weeks after Fred died, my father had a stroke. My dad had always been very healthy and self-sufficient, so this was completely unexpected. He was in three different hospitals while he recovered. Marci and Billy and I came together to figure out what would be the best situation for him when he got out of the hospital. We weren't sure if there were going to be any long-term effects of the stroke, but we knew he couldn't live by himself anymore. I started doing the research on local assisted living facilities. All of this was new information to me, and it was a lot to take in.

Of course, the regular routine of everyday life continues, no matter what we're going through. One evening I went to Brian's volleyball game at his school. The teams play several games, and when the teams switch sides, the fans switch sides in the bleachers. The coach's wife had just had a baby, so I was carrying a gift bag, my big purse, and my coat. I mustn't have been paying close enough attention while I was walking, because I tripped and fell right on my butt. There were a lot of people around and I was totally embarrassed. One of the dads helped me get up, and I kept saying, "I'm fine, don't worry," but my foot really hurt.

As the game went on, my foot started to swell, and I realized I couldn't even put weight on it. I didn't want to interrupt the game, so I waited until the end to flag down Brian. He and the helpful dad pretty much carried me to the car. The emergency room staff confirmed that it was broken, and the next day the doctor gave me a "boot" to walk around in and a pair of crutches.

It was my right foot, so I couldn't drive. But that didn't stop me from going with Marci to visit places for my dad. Greg drove me to visit my dad, and I kept working; I wasn't going to let a broken foot slow me down. We got my dad moved into his new place, hung pictures, and made it homey for him. Then one morning I woke up and my left ankle was swollen. I had favored my left foot so much that I sprained it; I was totally out of commission. I couldn't go anywhere or do anything but scoot around in a sitting position. I gave in. It was the only way I was going to heal.

It took about three months, but I eventually got my life back to normal. Or so I thought. I started having nightmares and anxiety attacks. I didn't feel right, although physically I was fine. I found myself replaying scenes from the divorce in my mind over and over again. I couldn't shake it. It made no sense to me, since this was all four years after the fact. Why was this happening now? Finally, a doctor friend of mine explained to me that I possibly could be going through PTSD. I had been in such a "coping" mode for so long—dealing with the divorce, a new marriage, being there for the kids, then moving, Fred's death, my dad's stroke, and my broken foot—that when things finally settled down my body was allowed to feel the stress. It hit me hard.

Robin F. Goodman, Ph.D., A.T.R.-BC, a licensed clinical psychologist and art therapist, says that it is important to be careful about what we label PTSD, which is a formal diagnosis based on specific reactions. To have it, someone must meet specific criteria. For example, PTSD can't be diagnosed before a month after the trauma, but the person can have the reaction later. The event must have involved "actual or threatened death or serious injury or threat to the physical integrity of the self or others...and the response involved intense fear, helplessness, or horror." Certain reactions—like arousal, re-experiencing, and avoidance—are also required.

Dr. Goodman explains that the end of a relationship is stressful because so many emotions come into play at once. "Depending on the circumstances—one may be having to deal with both the shock of the relationship being over or shock of how (e.g., a traumatic death) as well as feelings of sadness and intense longing. When relationships end—the most difficult of human experiences being when they end due to the death of someone—so much ends and changes, it's more than just the person not being there. When a relationship ends, it is stressful because of various changes and consequences."

Often, stress comes from not being able to trust after this experience. "There's a normal fear of further rejection or of a broken heart," Dr. Goodman says. "But once you've experienced a bad relationship, or the end of one, it can be scary to try again. Imagine eating something you thought was going to taste glorious—and perhaps it even did. Then one time you ate it, something somehow changed and it tasted horrible. You would be cautious about eating it again—remembering and having negative associations that may unfortunately overpower the positive memories and experiences. Therefore, to avoid further pain, you protect yourself by avoiding another relationship. The extreme example of this is in PTSD when the experience was so traumatic that there is a reliving of it and then one does things to avoid reminders of it."

Self-Care

One of the things that happens with PTSD is that the body's cortisol levels are all over the place. Cortisol has been termed the "stress hormone" because excess is secreted during times of physical or psychological stress, and the normal pattern of secretion can be altered. We can have too much cortisol, making us feel like we are in a state of stress all the time, even when we're not. To help even out our cortisol levels we need rest, protein, vitamins, and iron. It is extra important to eat healthy foods, get a good night's sleep, and take good care of ourselves.

We also need to spend time doing things that bring us joy. Joy builds up all those positive hormones that help us to feel good. It helps our body to remember what it feels like to feel good. Whatever it is—whether it's singing, dancing, playing with pets, visiting friends, laughing at movies, going to an amusement park, crafting, painting, doing volunteer work—whatever makes you happy, do that. Channel your emotions into activities that help you remember who you are.

Bodywork also helps a great deal in recovering from the effects of stress. Yes, a good massage feels great. And now there is research that shows just how healthy it is for us. So much so that many hospitals are making massage a part of their standard therapy. Researchers at the Group Health Center for Health Studies in Seattle say that massage works really well for relieving aches and pains. Massage reduces the stress hormone cortisol, while boosting our levels of serotonin and dopamine—so we feel good. When cortisol goes down, immune cells go up, so massage actually helps improve our immune systems. This also means less stress, less anxiety, and less depression. In addition, massage increases blood flow to the muscles, so that they can heal more easily. And massage can even help the pain caused by migraine headaches. A study at the Touch Research Institute showed that massage increases delta waves, making it easier for us to relax and fall asleep. They also found that massage helps to stimulate brain-wave activity, resulting in improved attention.

In Ayurveda there is a self-massage we can do called Abhyanga. It helps moisturize the skin, helps the skin to release toxins, and also helps to tone the muscles. The best part for stress relief is that it soothes the nervous system. Sesame oil is usually recommended in general, but other vegetable-based oils can be used. The massage can be done in the morning before your shower or in the evening before bed. Start by warming the oil to skin temperature, and drizzle a small amount of it into the palms of your hands. Massage the top of your scalp (on days when you wash your hair), paying particular attention to the circumference of your ears, and do the soles of your feet. Massage with long strokes on your limbs and round strokes on your joints. It's best to leave the oil on the body for twenty minutes before washing it off in a warm shower or bath.

Other bodywork techniques to help move energy through the body include acupuncture, acupressure, marma therapy, yoga, and reflexology.

Mind-set

It's no wonder we feel bad when a relationship changes, if we look at some of the labels and words associated with that particular change. The words death, divorce, breakup, failure, and "ex" all conjure up dark images. If we could adjust our vernacular to be more positive, more loving, then we might start to feel that way, too. Instead of death or dying, we could say passed on, or made the transition. Instead of divorce or breakup, we could say that we are redefining the relationship. After all, nothing is "broken." There is no "failure." Anything that happens in our lives leads us to where we are right now, which is exactly where we are supposed to be, where we agreed to be, need to be, and want to be. Things don't happen "to" us, we are participating in life.

The terms ex-husband and ex-wife sound so harsh—how about replacing "ex" with the word "former" instead? I usually refer to Jeff as Freddy and Brian's dad. Jeff and I have redefined our relationship. We are no longer spouses, but we continue to co-parent and we're still family. We have redefined our relationship in a way that we can communicate effectively, be friendly, and feel comfortable with the changes we've been through. This makes it easy for our kids to be comfortable too. It's a dramatic difference from the way things were when my own parents divorced.

At one point after I remarried, Lindsay dated Jeff for a little while. Friends would ask me if I thought that was weird, having my best friend date my former husband. But I thought it was great. If the two of them ever married I knew that my kids would have a great stepmother.

Steps and In-Laws

In our family there are a lot of "steps." I know first-hand what it means to have an extended family by marriage. When a new spouse comes into the picture, the family dynamics change again. We can all get along. For the kids, think of it as more love to go around—not competition for time or attention. When Greg moved in, he was very considerate of Freddy and Brian's feelings, and of Jeff's. Some people might think it's awkward or uncomfortable when we all sit together at a school volleyball game, but it's not. It really makes sense, and it's very natural. The kids call Greg by his first name, just like I do my stepfather.

Greg is from Australia, and his whole family is there. I was a little nervous to meet his mother, since I was basically taking her son to the other side of the world. But she embraced me, saw how happy Greg was, and was happy for both of us. Judith became "Mum" to me very quickly. We talked on the phone all the time. She came out for our wedding, and when Greg and I went to Australia we stayed at her house. It took me some time to develop a relationship with my stepchildren, mostly because they all live in Australia. We visited as much as we could, but what helped more than anything was e-mail. Phone calls aren't practical with the time difference, but we can easily keep up with each other's lives through e-mail. I feel very close to all three of them now. The miles don't matter.

Greg has a sister, Keri, who lives in Queensland. They were never very close, either geographically or personally, so I didn't have a chance to meet her until recently. When Judith passed away, we flew to Australia to help get the house in order and figure out all of the arrangements. I was a little nervous, since Greg and Keri had not spoken in more than five years. I didn't know what to expect. But we were all going through the same experience—having lost Judith and faced with the enormous task of organizing and distributing all of her things. It was quite emotional and a lot of hard work. Keri brought her middle son, Jason, and we all bonded quickly. I think we all understood how much Judith meant to us, and how much it would have meant to Judith to see us all working together so well.

Jason has a big heart. When Judith's neighbors came by, they all talked about how much they would miss her, and her beautiful garden that was her pride and joy. Jason took some of Judith's lovely rose bushes and replanted them in her friends' gardens so that they would have something to remember her by. It was a very touching gesture; Jason understood just how much that would have meant to his grandmother. It was a real tribute to her.

Judith kept a list of her best jewelry and how it was to be distributed. Unfortunately, several pieces were missing. We don't know if they were stolen or misplaced. One of the missing pieces was a pearl necklace that Judith had left to Keri. I could tell that Keri was upset about it. This was the one piece that really meant something special to her. I took the double strand of pearls that Judith left me and separated them so that we each had a single strand, and I gave Keri the strand with the clasp attached. She was very grateful, and I felt like this gesture brought us together as sisters. When we got home I had my pearls restrung, and every time I open my jewelry box I think about Keri, and how Judith brought us all together.

The Path to Understanding

- **Belief.** The first step on the path to understanding is belief. We need to believe that people are doing the best they can with the tools that they currently have. Jesus said: "Pray believing." I think this means we need to trust that somehow it's all going to work out.
- **Knowledge.** Our knowledge gives us strength. We can rely on what we know. We have to focus on that, and not on what we don't know, or what we speculate about.
- **Wisdom.** Knowledge, when accompanied by experience, gives us wisdom. And with wisdom comes growth.
- **Faith.** Faith is that calm inner-knowingness. Faith is unwavering.
- **Conviction.** Conviction is when we can embody the truth. It is truly understanding who we are, and expressing who we are without doubt or hesitation.

Notes

Transformation Applications

- Take care of your physical Self. Get a massage, exercise, go for a walk, do yoga. Experiment with bodywork like acupressure or acupuncture, the Alexander Technique, aromatherapy, etc. Eat healthy foods. Cut out junk foods. Practice mindful eating, rather than emotional eating.
- Take care of your emotional Self. Spend time with friends. Go to therapy. Find a support system. Allow yourself to cry when you need to. Do things that make you happy. Have fun!
- Take care of your spiritual Self. Meditate. Pray. Spend time in nature. Spend time with loved ones, including your pets.
- Take care of your intellectual Self. Read books. Go to museums. Challenge yourself with games and puzzles. Travel. Take a class.
- Take care of your environmental Self. Use canvas shopping and grocery bags. Use containers for your water rather than drinking from plastic bottles. Bring your own mug to work and to the coffee shop rather than using Styrofoam or cardboard cups. Drive less. Use energy-efficient appliances. De-clutter your closets—organize and give away or sell what you don't need or want. Feng Shui or Vastu your home and office.

Wisdom Affirmations for Understanding

- I understand that I may never be able to fully understand the purpose in this change, but that somehow, some way, it will all be OK.
- I understand that there is support and help available for me; I need only ask for it.
- I understand that there is a higher purpose behind any change and I trust that this change is for the best.

Chapter 9:
Integration

Self-trust is the first secret of success.
　　　　　　　　—Ralph Waldo Emerson

Robert Frost said that the only way to move on is to move through. Integration is about moving through. It's about integrating a change into your life so that you can move on from it positively. Don't *anticipate* what is going to happen—*participate* in what is going to happen! Create your future by being present and actively making decisions in the here and now.

Sometimes, living with a change in relationship means that we have to do things differently. We have to get out of our comfort zone. We might need to look deep within, reach out, call attention to ourselves, or even take risks. Ah, but with risks often come rewards!

Nine Lives or More

Vanessa Williams, one of my favorite actresses, said in an interview in *Parade Magazine*: "Every risk allows you to grow." This woman knows what she's talking about! She's an amazing example of reinvention, having taken every potentially negative situation she's been in, both personally and professionally, and not only learned and grown from it, but created something greater from it.

Vanessa has been married and divorced twice, and both marriages ended amid embarrassing rumors or her husbands' infidelity. How did she handle it? "I was shocked both times it happened to me. It hurt equally with each man. But I think eventually it helped me to feel more OK with myself and not to take things personally." Both of her former husbands continue to be an important part of the family, having holidays with their children and attending church together.

Thea Lobell, Ph.D., assistant professor at Louisiana State University Health Sciences Center, offers these tips for helping to let go of a relationship:

1) Take time to mourn the relationship along with future hopes and dreams with this relationship.
2) Engage in some kind of ritual to signify the end of the relationship: it can be as dramatic as writing down all of the hopes and dreams and burning them or as easy as erasing the person from one's speed dial. The key component is acting in a mindful way, acknowledging that this relationship is over.

And to maintain a civil relationship when this person is still in your life because of work or family:

1) Remember this person is your ex for a reason.
2) Focus on the positive aspects that drew you to this person.
3) Craft your time together where there is less likely to be conflict.

Déjà Vu?

The theory behind reincarnation is that after death the soul comes back to live another life and learn more lessons. I have found that oftentimes we live more than one life in this very lifetime. We have several opportunities for new beginnings as time goes on. When I left home for college, and then entered the working world, I felt like a new person, with new opportunities and new relationships in front of me. Getting married and starting a family with Jeff was another new life for me. And then, after the divorce and the second marriage, came another beginning. Now that my boys are away at school themselves, starting their own lives and careers, it's also a beginning for me. I have integrated these changes into my life, and it has given me more freedom in my choices. I miss going to the volleyball games, but I don't miss the school fund-raisers, carpools, or staying on top of homework and all that. I can travel, I can write more, and I can volunteer more.

I look at other women my age as amazing examples of how to live life courageously and integrate the changes that come along in our lives. Sheryl Crow's songs are inspiring and life-affirming. She is creative and resilient. And she also had to find closure at least one time in her life. Sheryl went through a high-profile engagement and breakup and just six days later was diagnosed with breast cancer. She moved through it by allowing herself to feel the pain, and the fear, deal with it and release it, rather than distracting herself by staying busy. She explained in an interview in *Parade Magazine* that this process helped her become more awake and aware:

"It helped me to remember who I am." Now she is healthy and stronger than ever, and a new relationship has her focused on both motherhood and the environment. She adopted a baby boy and is passionate about issues such as global warming. "When a baby comes into your life, the environment becomes so personal. Having him around, this little innocent spirit, really made me fearless about writing what I wanted to write… It created a lot of urgency about that."

Ann Curry, of *NBC News* and *The Today Show*, said in an article for *MORE Magazine*: "Losing my brother at a young age has given me the privilege of knowing that I don't have a lot of time. I want to spend it well." Ann has certainly spent her time well, traveling to Darfur and reporting on the crisis there, forging a career in a demanding field, and also living a happy family life with her husband and children. She told me that she learned this fortitude from her mother, who taught her of the Japanese word *gambaru*. Gambaru means: "Never give up, no matter what, always do your best." This has been a theme in her life that has given her strength through hard times. Although Ann misses her mother deeply, she takes this lesson very much to heart, and with gratitude. It is one way she has integrated what her mother taught her into her life.

Sometimes, when we're going through a change in relationship, we lose ourselves. We're so focused on what is changing that we forget what is staying the same. People come and go from our lives, but we are still here! We have everything we need within ourselves. We have the strength, the resources, and the intelligence not only to survive, but to thrive. When we come through the pain we remember who we are. Our relationships may change, the roles we play may change, but we are still the same unique, amazing expression of spirit that we always were, and always will be.

We can look for closure from someone else, from outside of ourselves, but we will never find it there. It comes only from ourselves. No one can do it for us. We have to do the work; we have to go through the process. We can't let ourselves get distracted from what is important, which is our own inner peace. And there are so many distractions to take us away from ourselves. The computer, TV, and work are just a few. We can be so successful at distracting ourselves that the distractions turn into addictions. We end up hurting ourselves more than we were hurt by the change in relationship. Henry David Thoreau said: "In proportion as our inward life fails, we go more constantly and desperately to the post office. You may depend on it, that poor fellow who walks away with the greatest number of letters, proud of his extensive correspondence, has not heard from himself this long while." If you find yourself drifting away from yourself, pay attention.

It is important to face our fears, to look at where we are hurting and work through it. It doesn't serve us to avoid the pain, resist it, or hide from it. Check in with yourself. Feel the emotions; process them. It might be guilt, relief, anger, shame, resentment, or a mix of emotions. You will get through it; you are stronger than you think you are. It is better to understand what we can learn from the experience, and integrate the knowledge that comes from it into our lives. When we do this, we can make better choices for ourselves, coming from a higher perspective and seasoned wisdom.

The Rest of the Story

After Fred passed away, Marci was understandably distraught and under a lot of stress. There she was, at just forty-two years old, a widow with two teenagers. Many people in this circumstance would fall apart, but Marci called on her inner strength, and she kept it together. She gave a moving eulogy at Fred's funeral, and made sure that her kids had everything they needed to get through this very trying time. She continued to move forward, going back to work, helping out with our dad, and spending time with her mother-in-law. It helped that Marci had a strong support system in her family, Fred's family, and her friends and neighbors.

A few months after things started to settle down, Marci decided to host a backyard barbecue for her neighbors, to thank them for helping her out so much. She put herself out there; she took a risk. Marci loves to entertain and she's really good at it, so having a party like this is really a form of therapy for her. Her neighborhood is very close-knit, and she wanted to bring everyone together to show her gratitude, and to enjoy each other again after so much sadness. She invited everybody, including her neighbor from two doors down, a man she had met but didn't know. It turned out that just three months before Marci lost Fred, Steve had lost his wife, Candy, to cancer. He had spent the previous two years taking care of her while still working as a doctor, so he hadn't gotten to know the other neighbors. He was grateful to be invited to Marci's, and offered to take her out to dinner to thank her.

Marci and Steve were both going through similar experiences having lost their spouses, and they spent a long time talking. They were able to help each other integrate back into life. They walked their dogs together and got to know each other as friends. Little by little, the friendship turned to love. And to make a long story short, Steve and Marci ended up getting married. At the wedding, held in Steve's brother's backyard, the rabbi talked about how Fred and Candy were very much present and blessing this union. And I think we all felt it. Marci keeps photos of Fred and Candy in their family room. Steve and Marci have moved on with their lives, but they haven't left their pasts behind. They have successfully integrated what they learned in their relationships and their marriages to build a life together.

Marci thinks the whole scenario is like a Lifetime TV movie, to go from such tragedy to a new, happy beginning for both families that have come together. Steve had a ready-made family with Marci's kids. A. J. gave a wonderful toast at the wedding. Emma calls her new stepfather "Pop."

Christine's Story

Christine was the same age as Emma, fourteen, when her father died. He had been sick for two years, and although she and her brother, Carlton, and their mother knew this was coming, it was still hard to deal with. Their mother reconnected with one of her former boyfriends, and moved the family from Rhode Island to California so that she could be with him. Christine had to cope with another huge change, and make new friends in a completely new city. She ended up going back to Rhode Island for college, but after graduation she returned to California to be near her mother and brother. Not long after Christine married Joe, her mother passed away.

Carlton and Christine had always been close, but the experience of losing both of their parents bonded them even more. Christine and Joe had their two children, and finally Uncle Carlton married Adrienne and bought a home close by so that they could all hang out together.

But then, just a year after the wedding, Carlton suddenly got sick and was diagnosed with a rare form of brain cancer. He died very quickly. Christine lost her brother, Adrienne lost her husband, and Joe lost his best friend. All three of them came together to help each other through this tough time. Adrienne will always be family to Joe and Christine. She is Aunt Adrienne to their kids and is very much present in their lives. Adrienne has remarried and now has a child of her own, and Christine is the baby's godmother. They've been able to integrate all the changes into their lives and continue to share the love they have for Carlton with each other. It is because of Carlton that they all came together.

Carlton is with his family in the love they have for each other. He is there in his sister's resilience and optimism. He is there with Joe, sharing his enthusiasm during the UCLA game. He's with Adrienne, loving and appreciating her kindness and generosity. He's in his nephew's outgoingness and his niece's determination.

Continuity

Pamela Waitkus, Ed.S., a licensed marriage and family counselor, says that after a divorce you still need to have a relationship with your ex. "You have a child/children together that need attention, love and nurturing. I would like to think that people could sit down and talk about how to raise their children, schedules of activities, etc., but often that is not the case. I recommend counseling for the parents so that they begin talking to each other regarding the children and stop arguing. If the parents are able to talk then that is what they need to be doing about everything from how to tell the children we are not living together, to visitation and childcare to how to discipline and set boundaries. It takes effort that will pay off not only for the parents but for the children as well."

She offers up these tips for divorced parents:

1. Listening is the most important thing to learn how to do with each other. So often people get defensive and feel attacked; try to keep the emotion out of the discussion.
2. Recognize you will be dealing with the other parent for the rest of your life—you are a parent forever, like it or not.

3. Show respect for the other person; your children continue to learn valuable lessons from you on how to have a healthy or unhealthy relationship.
4. When issues or concerns come up talk with the other parent immediately so that you can be on the same page with the child.
5. Present a united front with the child. Kids can take advantage of the situation and play parent against parent.
6. Remember you can be a great mother or father without being married to the person!

Releasing

Part of integrating a change into our life is moving forward. In life, we can't be in two places at the same time. We can't keep both feet on the ground and expect to go anywhere. If we want to take that leap of faith, and really make changes in our lives, then both feet have to leave the ground. How can we do this? We need to release. We need to let go. A caterpillar lets go of life as a caterpillar to become a butterfly. An acorn sprouts to become a tree.

Think of it this way. When you're in high school, you can apply to college, write the essay, fill out the application, get the recommendation, and even receive a letter of acceptance. But what needs to happen? You still need to graduate from high school before you can actually attend a university. All the other tasks won't help at all unless you follow through and get that diploma. So we need to finish it. We need to let go. We can't be a caterpillar and a butterfly at the same time. If we want to fly, we need to commit.

The Releasing Prayer

Dear God, Sweet Spirit,

Knowing that all is one and I am one with all that is—

I recognize that certain habits, or thought patterns, or misconceptions

No longer serve me, no longer contribute to my greatest good.

I choose, here and now, to release any and all

judgments, anger, guilt, or self-destructive behaviors.

I choose to let go of pain, and heartache, to let go of resentment and blame.

I choose to unburden myself of any heaviness that is weighing me down.

I choose to leave behind any pettiness of the past.

I choose to relinquish control, to let You,

the guiding light of the Universe, in Your infinite Wisdom,

take care of the details of my life.

I choose to open the door, to clear out the clutter, in my life and in my mind, and to make room for

All that is offered to me.

I choose to let go completely—and let GOD!

I choose, right here and now, to give up the struggle.

I choose, right here and now, to release all my fears, all my doubts, any falsehoods that are holding me back from knowing and experiencing and celebrating all that I am.

I choose to get with the program, to embrace the

Trust and Faith, and Health, and Light, and Truth, and Opportunity, and Love, and Prosperity and Wholeness

That right here and now runs in and around and through each and every one of us. This is who I am.

And I am truly grateful.

I now release and let go of anything that contradicts this fact. Whatever it is, I let it go. Happily, with grace and ease, and forever.

And so it is, baby—and so it absolutely is!

Amen!

Another Tool

There is a saying in the Indian texts: "When you let go a little, you get a little happiness. When you let go a lot, you get a lot of happiness. And when you let go completely, you get FREEDOM." One tool I've found very useful in helping to attain emotional freedom is hypnotherapy. Dick Sutphen is a hypnotherapist who will often do past-life regressions to help people look at their relationships and figure out what karma, or past experiences, have led to their current situations. You can look at what experiences you've shared with another person to better understand what brought you together. When you can understand the cause of the situation, you can release the effect that it is having on you. You can release the pain, fear, anger, guilt, or whatever emotion you are feeling as a result of the relationship—and forgive. You can forgive this person in your life, and you can also forgive yourself. Forgiveness is a gift you give to yourself. And by forgiving, you set yourself free.

To Be Continued

Integration is understanding what we've been through and moving through it. It is taking with us what we've learned, and living our lives with these new insights. Integration allows us to be wiser, more loving, and more aware, and it opens us up to gratitude.

Notes:

Transformation Applications

- How do you distract yourself? What are you avoiding healing? Look at any pain or anger or hurt and feel it, deal with it.
- Be conscious of any words that follow "I am." Do not define yourself by your anger, fear, or pain. You are not angry. You may *feel* angry, but that is not who you are.
- Where do you find your Self? How do you remember your Self?
- Don't anticipate, *participate*. How can you participate in productive activities? How can you channel your time and energy into productive activity?

Wisdom Affirmations for Integration

- I move through life with purpose and fluidity.
- Every experience I have been through has gone to shape the person I am today. I learn and grow as a result of change.
- I take what I have learned with me and I am equipped to handle challenges that come my way.

Chapter 10:
Gratitude

Change your thoughts, and in the twinkling of an eye, all your conditions change. Your world is a world of crystallized ideas, crystallized words. Sooner or later, you reap the fruits of your words and thoughts.
                                    —Florence Scovel Shinn

The last step to closure is Gratitude. Having gratitude means that we can look back at the relationship without anger or hurt. We can think about it when we want to, and see the gifts in it. We can look at the growth that we received from the relationship, and the blessings, and be grateful for all of it.

Gratitude is connected to forgiveness, and yet is more profound. Having learned and grown from the relationship, it is saying in your heart: "Thank you for giving me this experience." It is acknowledging that everything right now is all "right" because everything is as it is supposed to be. We recognize the fulfilled agreement and can move on, knowing that we are perfectly whole, complete, and perfect.

Yes Man

In the movie *Yes Man,* Jim Carrey plays a man who is still basically grieving a past relationship. He's resigned himself to a lonely life, saying no to friends and opportunities. But one day this finally gets old for him, and he reaches out for help. He attends a seminar where he is convinced to say yes to any chance that comes along. At first, he does this because he has to. But as time goes on, and he sees his life really change for the better, he understands that he does have the power of choice, and that when he chooses to say yes, good things can happen. So he starts saying yes when he wants to, with no fear, and no expectations—just an awareness of the infinite possibilities. Gratitude opens up your heart to embrace new opportunities. Say yes and see what happens.

Passion and Enthusiasm

Steve Irwin, the wildlife expert and television host known as "The Crocodile Hunter," died when he was pierced in the chest with a stingray barb in 2006. He was just forty-four years old. Steve had said in interviews that he always wanted to be remembered for his "passion and enthusiasm." He was certainly passionate about animals, and conservation, and he lived his life with great enthusiasm, and it showed on camera. He left behind his wife, Terri, and their two children. In an interview with Barbara Walters shortly after his death, Terri said, "I feel blessed. I had the best fourteen years. A romance I didn't think was possible."

Terri Irwin is an excellent example of gratitude in action. She continues her husband's work as a wildlife conservationist, and encourages her children to pursue their own passions. As fans we grieved Steve's death too, but we need to be grateful for his life. He made so many contributions to this world during his time here. He will be remembered, and loved, always.

Retirement

In September 2006, tennis great Andre Agassi played his last tournament, retiring at the U.S. Open at age thirty-six. His fans helped him to find closure with this decision. He received a standing ovation from a crowd of more than twenty thousand people. Among the crowd showing their love were his wife, Steffi Graf, and their two children. Moved to tears, Andre said, "The scoreboard said I lost today, but what the scoreboard doesn't say is what I have found... You have pulled for me on the court and also in life. I found inspiration." The crowd showed their gratitude to Andre that day. The relationship changed, because he wouldn't be on the courts playing anymore, but the memories remain. This was a historic day.

Present Moment Awareness

When we are in gratitude, we are in the present moment. We're not dwelling on the past, or worried about the future, we're simply in the here and now. Robert Emmons has studied gratitude scientifically. He's a professor of psychology at the University of California, Davis. His studies have proven that the practice of gratitude can increase happiness levels by around 25 percent. In addition to this, he's found that cultivating gratitude brings other health benefits, such a longer and better quality of sleep. So, gratitude is good for us in many wonderful ways.

Melodie Beattie, author of *Codependent No More*, says: "Gratitude unlocks the fullness of life. It turns what we have into enough, and more. It turns denial into acceptance, chaos into order, confusion into clarity... It turns problems into gifts, failures into success, the unexpected into perfect timing, and mistakes into important events. Gratitude makes sense of our past, brings peace for today and creates a vision for tomorrow."

The Sand Mandala

The sand mandala is a Tibetan Buddhist tradition involving the creation and also destruction of mandalas made from colored sand. I had the pleasure of watching this all happen during my trip to India. In the ritual, a group of monks create an elaborate and very intricately designed piece of art using colored sand. The artwork holds much symbolism, and is geometrically laid out in detail. It can take days, and even weeks to build the mandala, as each monk uses special tools to pour the sand in just the right way to create the design. They start from the center and move outward, and usually work in shifts around the clock. They work quietly, with much concentration and attention. It is quite intense, and absolutely beautiful with all of the colors.

Once the mandala is complete, it is surrounded by candles, and there is often chanting performed around it. This is when we stand in awe at the beauty of this mandala, when we take in its beauty, and express gratitude for having witnessed it. And then, in a very ritualistic ceremony, one monk stands and sweeps the mandala away. All of the sand blends together. The design is gone, the colors merge to become a kind of tan and gray, and we are left with a pile of sand. The destruction of the mandala is done as a metaphor of the impermanence of life. It is a reminder to us to appreciate and be grateful for what is before us while it is there. It is a symbol of the Buddhist doctrinal belief in the transitory nature of material life.

The sand is swept up and placed in an urn. Half of the sand is distributed to those watching the closing ceremony. I have a little vial of sand that I kept to remember this experience. The other half is carried to a nearby body of water, where it is deposited. The waters then carry the healing blessing to the ocean, and from there is spreads throughout the world for planetary healing. So although the mandala, in all its glory, is no longer physically present, it still serves a very important purpose. Nothing is ever wasted. The repercussions are felt far and wide. The gifts continue to flow. And for that we can be grateful.

Thank You

I have learned to find gratitude in my own life. As difficult as it was on me at the time, I am grateful for the experience of my parents' divorce. It helped me to become who I am today. I can see how it was better for my parents, so I am grateful for that. I am grateful that we moved because I got to meet people I never would have met otherwise, and cultivated amazing friendships that I learned and grew from. And as my parents get older, I am grateful that I can now help them, and get to know them as friends rather than just parents.

I am grateful to Jeff for the years we spent together. I am grateful for the two children that we have. Jeff and I really grew up together. We married so young, and

I don't think either of us really knew who we were yet, but we helped each other find out. And I am grateful that we were able to change our relationship to one that is better for us now. I am grateful for all the opportunities we have had to learn and grow from our relationship.

I am grateful that Marci and Fred had the time together that they had. I am grateful for their two children, my beautiful niece and nephew. It was when Fred was dying that I came up with the idea for this book. That whole experience helped me to understand the importance of closure, and to process and formulate just how we go about getting closure. Fred gave me many gifts in his life, but the greatest gift was the gift of his friendship.

I am grateful that I was able to know my grandparents, and learn from their wisdom and experience. I am grateful that my two grandmothers got to know my children, and that they could see themselves reflected in their great-grandchildren.

I think of all the people I have known and loved in this lifetime, who have now left this earth—and I am grateful that each and every one of them was a part of my life.

I think of all the friends I had that drifted away for one reason or another, and I am grateful for the time we had together. Each person added something to my life; each person taught me something in some way. We're all here to help each other, and I know we did that— that our agreement was fulfilled.

Cultivating Gratitude

When thankfulness o'erflows the swelling heart, and breathes in free and uncorrupted praise for benefits received, propitious Heaven takes such acknowledgement as fragrant incense, and doubles all its blessings.

—Lillo

There are many ways we can cultivate gratitude and make gratitude a part of our lives every day. Here are a few suggestions:

Gratitude journal. Keep a blank book by the side of your bed. When you wake up, start your day by writing down three to five things you are grateful for. While you are writing, really feel the emotion; let gratitude fill your heart, and take time to really think about what you are writing. It's nice to have this book to refer to, so that you can look back and read what you wrote on previous days. As an alternative, you can keep a journal on your computer. First thing after you turn it on, before you check your e-mail or get to work, write the three to five things that you are grateful for in this journal. Starting the day with gratitude sets the tone for the day and helps to remind us of what is really important.

Thank-you notes. We know that it is good manners to write thank-you notes when someone has given us a present. It also makes the recipient feel appreciated. But we can also write thank-you notes just to show our gratitude for having the person in our life. It helps us to recognize the goodness in people, and how much our relationships mean to us. And receiving thank-you notes is wonderful! I have a file on my computer where

I keep thank-you notes from my subscribers. Hearing from people in this way means the world to me. So, if I can make that impact on others by expressing gratitude to them, I definitely want to do it. Alfred Painter said: "Saying thank you is more than good manners, it is good spirituality."

Pay attention. There is so much to be grateful for. But are we paying attention? We often pay attention to what we don't have instead of what we do have. Look at that gas tank as half full, instead of stressing that you're already on half empty. Be grateful for the job that you have to wake up for, instead of being irritated that you have to set the alarm clock. Be grateful for the sun when it shines, and also for the rain that waters our thirsty earth. Let life's beauty inspire you to feel gratitude.

Prayers. Meister Eckhart said: "If the only prayer you said in your whole life was 'thank you,' that would suffice." As we begin our day in gratitude, so we may also end our day in gratitude. Give thanks for the day, for the lessons learned, for the people you interacted with, and that you have another opportunity to be grateful in the morning.

Conscious choice making. Many times things happen and we react. We don't take time to think about our reaction, we just act out of instinct. But we have to remember that we do have choices, and we can choose again. For example, someone cuts us off in traffic. Our instinct might be to get angry, lash out, or be frustrated. But if we stop a moment and think, we see that there are other choices for us. First of all, we can be grateful that we didn't get in an accident. We also can understand that this person did not mean to cut us off; he or she did not do it intentionally. We don't have to take the action personally. We might even guess that the person is stressed out, and not paying attention as well as he or she should. We can have compassion for that person, and send him or her light and love. We also might see that the person did us a favor, because by cutting us off we arrived at our destination at exactly the right time to meet someone we really wanted to meet. Everything happens for a reason, so we actually can be grateful to that person.

Naikan. *Naikan* is a form of Buddhist meditation developed by Yoshimoro Ishin of the Jodo Shinshu sect in Japan. Naikan means "introspection." It is poetically translated to mean: "seeing oneself with the mind's eye." This is a structured method of self-reflection that helps us to understand ourselves, and relationships, and our own human nature. Naikan is practiced to cultivate gratitude. The idea is to help us look at the big picture, to see things we hadn't noticed before. There are three questions which make up the Naikan meditation. In the blank spaces, fill in the names of people in your life.

1. What have I received from _____?
2. What have I given to _____?
3. What troubles and difficulties have I caused _____?

It can be very simple, looking at the day, or more intricate, looking at the lifetime of a relationship. For example, for the first question, I might say about this morning: My husband gave me a kiss good morning. My cat gave me a cuddle. My car (OK, not a person, but I am still grateful that I have my Prius to get around in) successfully took me to the chiropractor's. My chiropractor gave me a great adjustment. My friend gave me a phone call. These are all things that I can be grateful for. We don't look at the person's attitude or motivation, because that does not change the fact that we benefited from this person's effort.

For the second question, we look at the other side of the equation. It is important to see a balance, to be conscious of our own level of giving. We do not need to worry if we are giving too much—because if we give with the expectation of getting something in return we stress ourselves out, and defeat the purpose of giving from the heart. But we need to show appreciation and gratitude for the things that other people do for us. We do not want to take someone's efforts for granted.

In the third question, we look at how we have caused someone inconvenience or difficulty. More often, we tend to look at what other people did to cause us difficulty, like the person cutting us off in traffic. But we need to look at ourselves and our actions, and take responsibility for how we treat other people. This is a very Buddhist concept, reflecting on ourselves and our behavior to more fully know ourselves.

More Self-Reflection

Benjamin Franklin practiced a form of daily self-reflection. He developed a list of thirteen virtues, and each day he would evaluate his own conduct relative to a particular virtue. We can translate from old English to understand that we must encourage moderation in all things, to be true to our word, to do good work, and to be kind to others. He wrote the following list in 1741:

Benjamin Franklin's Thirteen Virtues

1. **Temperance:** Eat not to dullness; drink not to elevation.
2. **Silence:** Speak not but what may benefit others or yourself; avoid trifling conversation.
3. **Order:** Let all your things have their places; let each part of your business have its time.
4. **Resolution:** Resolve to perform what you ought; perform without fail what you resolve.
5. **Frugality:** Make no expense but to do good to others or yourself; i.e., waste nothing.
6. **Industry:** Lose no time; be always employ'd in something useful; cut off all unnecessary actions.
7. **Sincerity:** Use no hurtful deceit; think innocently and justly, and, if you speak, speak accordingly.
8. **Justice:** Wrong none by doing injuries, or omitting the benefits that are your duty.
9. **Moderation:** Avoid extremes; forbear resenting injuries so much as you think they deserve.
10. **Cleanliness:** Tolerate no uncleanliness in body, cloaths, or habitation.
11. **Tranquility:** Be not disturbed by trifles, or at accidents common or unavoidable.

12. **Chastity:** Rarely use venery but for health or offspring, never to dullness, weakness, or the injury of your own or another's peace or reputation.

13. **Humility:** Imitate Jesus and Socrates.

Benjamin Franklin also said: "Be in general virtuous, and you will be happy."

When we are happy, we have no resentments, no blame, no fear—just gratitude. And when we have gratitude for a relationship, then we can have closure. It all comes back to our relationship with our Self.

Notes:

Transformation Applications

- How can I begin the day in gratitude?
- How can I end the day in gratitude?
- How can I remind myself to feel grateful during the day?
- What can I do to express gratitude to the people in my life?
- In what ways can I express gratitude for my life? How can I live as an example to others?
- What am I grateful for in each of the relationships in my life?

Wisdom Affirmations for Gratitude

- I am grateful for the people who have had an impact on my life.
- I am grateful for the experiences that have had an impact on my life.
- I am grateful for myself, my strength, compassion, and capacity for love.

Part 3

Reconnection

Chapter 11:
Coming Full Circle

I was always looking outside myself for strength and confidence, but it comes from within. It is there all the time.

—Anna Freud

The Law of Relationship says that we are all connected. And what connects us is Spirit. And so here we are. Right where we started, right where we've always been. Our relationships may have changed, our roles may have changed, but we are still here. Sometimes, we need to remember who we are; we need a reminder or two in order to keep things in perspective. We need to feel that connection with spirit, to sort of plug in and recharge our batteries.

Reminders

We can find that reminder in nature. Fresh air, blue sky, trees, animals. It doesn't matter if you live in the desert or the mountains or near the ocean. It doesn't matter if you live on a farm, in the city, or in suburbia. We all feel the same sunshine; we all see the same moon. We each have opportunities to spend time in nature. When we spend time in nature we get closer to our own nature. Away from distractions, we have time to regroup and relax.

Look at the examples that nature gives us. The seasons change effortlessly. When autumn comes, the tree doesn't mourn and try to get the leaves to reattach themselves. When the baby ducks leave home, the parents don't run after them. And when the baby ducks grow up they don't move back home with their laundry! Change is natural; change is inevitable. Sometimes it's a breeze, and sometimes it's an earthquake, and yet nature manages to heal itself.

In silence, we can find that reminder of who we are. When we turn off the TV, step away from the computer, get away from all the gossip and chatter and just sit with ourselves, we can hear it. We can hear that voice within, we can hear that higher wisdom, we can listen to our heart. The song in our heart is love. It's all love. That's who we are.

When we know who we are, we are true to ourselves and it shows. When Brian was in the ninth grade he had an English assignment where he had to write a paper choosing one word to describe one of his parents. The word he chose for me was "authentic." To this day, that is the best compliment I've ever gotten. Who we are authentically is so beautiful that there is no need to try to be anything else. Each one of us has it in us; we just have to remember it.

We can find that reminder of who we are in our spiritual practices. There is no one size fits all. Whatever brings you joy, and peace, whatever lets you experience more fully who you are, that is how you connect with spirit. Prayer, meditation, chanting, contemplation, study, service, yoga—whatever it is, it's all good. Even the work we do can be a spiritual practice. When we find work that we love, and that helps people in some way, we have found our dharma, our purpose in life. And that is a beautiful thing.

For most of us, knowing who we are does not necessarily come in one big "lightbulb" moment. It happens gradually, over time, as we learn and grow. When I was thirteen years old, my mother had a friend who ran a summer camp in Utah. She made a deal with him to do the accounting for the camp so that my brother and sister and I could attend. This was our first time away from home, not at a relative's house, and it was a real adventure. Utah is incredibly beautiful, and getting out in nature was exactly what we all needed to help us heal from the stresses at home.

Survival

Each week we broke up into smaller groups for various outings. One week I went with a group on a houseboat, water-skiing on Lake Powell. Another week we went horseback riding and camped out in pup tents. The third week, rather than stay in camp and do arts and crafts, I decided to tag along with the older girls and go on "survival training."

There were six girls and three counselors on the trip. A bus dropped us off in the desert, and we were to follow a dry riverbed, walking five miles a day for five days to reach our pickup location on the final day. We each carried with us an army blanket rolled up with straps to make a backpack. Inside the blanket, we each had one little bag of raisins, one little bag of flour, one little bag of dried milk, and one little bag of nuts. We had a canteen of water, and the wooden spoons we carved ourselves. And we also got a couple of matches. The idea was to ration carefully and find our food and shelter in the desert. We also took a journal to record our thoughts about things.

This was summer, so it was definitely hot in the desert. We only had the clothes that we wore, so we were instructed to dress in layers because it gets very cold at night. Anyone who knows me knows that I am definitely not the camping type, and I certainly wasn't back then either. I borrowed my sister's hiking boots for this trek through the desert.

There were many lessons to learn all along the way. With no other entertainment, we talked and talked, and sang songs, and wrote in our journals. I learned how to make a fire. I learned how to make "ash cakes"—our desert delicacy. We would mix a little of the flour with a little of the water and shape the dough into a patty. Then, the patty went right on the hot ashes to cook. Flip it over, dust off the ashes, and dinner is served! When I wanted to get really gourmet I'd add a couple of my precious raisins to the mix. One time I was mixing my dough and it just wouldn't get thick—I kept adding flour, but it wasn't working. I finally figured out that I was using my powdered milk by mistake.

Most nights we slept under the stars, but one night we felt really lucky to find a kind of carved-out cave in the side of a big rock. We huddled together in the cave and were especially warm that night. The next morning, we woke up with mosquito bites everywhere! We had encroached on the territory of someone else's "home."

The walking wasn't bad. The terrain was basically flat, and we were following the riverbed so we couldn't get lost. The counselors would take turns staying up at night to keep the fire going, and we were all together so I felt safe. The Law of Relationship says we are here to help each other. And each of us played a part in getting the rest of us through this experience.

On our last night in the desert, the counselors told us what a great job we had done, and that as our "graduation" we each were going to go "solo." That meant spending the night alone, all by myself, in the desert. They would drop us off a half mile apart, one by one, and we would find our way back to the last one dropped off in the morning. Since I was the youngest, I was dropped off first. One of the counselors gave me some extra matches "just in case." This was a huge challenge and I was scared, but I was willing to go through with it.

As the girls hiked away, I got to work on my fire. It was frustrating trying to do this all on my own, but I managed. I didn't mind spending time by myself—I've always been fine alone. But as it started to get dark, and cold, the world suddenly felt very big, and I felt very vulnerable. I heard this unfamiliar sound, and it got louder and louder. A kind of rumbling, and it was coming from the river. I could barely make out that its water was now flowing very quickly. It wasn't raining, and I didn't know where it was coming from, but it was enough to convince me to bundle up my gear and start hiking toward the next girl up. I no longer wanted to be alone!

I started howling our "aaaah-ooooh" signal—a sound that is supposed to carry farther across the desert. As I walked along the river, I could tell the water was rising. I heard the faint "aaaah-ooooh" answered back and ran toward it. It was my friend, and she was on the other side of the river. I could see her campfire, big and bright, so much bigger and brighter than mine had been. The river was now rushing, and I knew I had to cross it to get to her. I waded in, and was surprised to find that the water was up to my waist. It was difficult getting across while the water pushed me sideways, but my friend was there to lend me a hand on the other side. She helped pull me up and out and sat me by the fire to dry off.

The noise from the river was so loud that we could barely hear another cry of "aaaah-ooooh." We howled back. It was another girl, coming from the other direction. Luckily, she was on the same side of the river, so she didn't have to cross it. The three of us huddled together. I was soaked. I took Marci's shoes off and set them by the fire to dry.

At some point we must have fallen asleep, because the next thing I remember was opening my eyes to daylight and hearing a chorus of "aaaah-ooooh." The rest of our group was looking for us. We shared our stories and the counselors explained that we had experienced a flash flood. This was our last day of hiking, and we were all eager to get back to camp—to showers and food. I went to put on Marci's shoes and found that they were burned to a crisp. There was no way I could get them on my feet, so I walked the rest of the way in my socks.

For all our chatter throughout the trip, during the ride home we were silent. Exhausted, talked-out, dirty, and hungry, we arrived at camp to be greeted by Marci and Billy and all the other kids. The look on Marci's face when she saw me was one I will never forget—sheer horror and relief, at the same time. "You survived!" she said.

Yes, I survived. And although I have never again had any desire to go camping in any way, shape, or form, I know that if I could get through that experience, I can get through anything. College? Marriage? Kids? Divorce? Death? I can do it. Life is not just about surviving; it's about living. It's about participating, and getting every ounce of experience you can out of it. If that means having to go through some changes in relationships—that's OK. Because the relationship itself is so valuable, so precious, no matter what context it comes in, that the benefits far outweigh anything else that comes with it. I found my strength, I felt that spirit, and I know that it is always there, in any circumstance.

Transcendence

Fast-forward to about twenty-six years later. I'm in India on a trip with my dear friend and teacher Deepak Chopra and about five hundred other people from all around the world. We just got back from visiting the Taj Mahal and we're at the hotel, sitting on a beautiful lawn outside. Deepak and his father are participating in a traditional Buddhist ceremony with the Shankracharya, the spiritual leader and holy man. They are chanting in Sanskrit, and throwing rose petals and offerings into a fire. The fire grows higher and higher, the chanting becomes hypnotic, and the air is filled with an exotic fragrance. I'm sitting there thinking that this moment is so magical I want to remember it always, to carry this feeling I have with me now forever. In the distance, I see a man walking a camel and a young boy perched on top enjoying the ride. I think—how perfect, how beautiful, how wonderful. My friend leans over and points out the same thing I'm seeing and asks, "Isn't that Freddy on the camel?" Yes! It is Freddy, my son! Just when I was thinking things couldn't get any more remarkable, they absolutely did.

That's Life

And that's life. One day we can be walking in the desert with no shoes, dirty, and hungry. And another day we can be a witness to something so amazing it takes our breath away. We're still the same person through all of it. One day we can be walking down the aisle with flowers and promises, and another day we're picking up the pieces of a broken heart. A little older, a little wiser, but we're still the same soul through all of it. Know who you are, and love yourself through all of it.

Pablo Casals

When I was sixteen, I went to my first self-growth type of class. It was an interesting time for me, having just gotten my first job and feeling independent and self-sufficient. At the end of the weekend we were given a piece of paper, and written on it was this quote by the Spanish cellist Pablo Casals. I framed that piece of paper and still have it in my office today. It has helped inform everything I do. Here it is:

Each second we live is a new and unique moment of the universe, a moment that never was before and never will be again. And what do we teach our children? We teach that 2 + 2 make 4 and that Paris is the capital of France. When will we also teach them what they are? We should say to each of them: Do you know what you are? You are a marvel. You are unique. In all the world there is no other child exactly like you. In the millions of years that have passed there has never been a child like you. And look at your body—what a wonder it is! Your legs and your arms, your cunning fingers, the way you move. You may become a Shakespeare, a Michelangelo, a Beethoven. You have the capacity for anything. Yes, you are a marvel. And when you grow up, can you then harm another who is, like you, a marvel? You must cherish one another. You must work—we must all work—to make this world worthy of its children.

—*Pablo Casals*

Shine Through

When I was going through that awkward teenage stage, I came up with my own kind of mantra to help keep me centered and on track, despite all the "stuff" going on around me both at home and at school. "SHINE THROUGH." I wrote it on a piece of paper and taped it to my closet door, so that I would see it prominently in my room every day. To me it was a sign to remember who I am. To remember that there is a light inside me that burns bright, no matter what is going on outside of me.

I'm not that awkward teenager anymore. I've learned from my experiences and from my relationships with other people. I'm living my life and growing as I go, both accepting and honoring the growing pains. I have gratitude for all the relationships that come and go, as well as for the relationship that I have, and always will have, with myself.

Let your light shine.

Notes:

Transformation Applications

- Spend time with yourself. Romance yourself. Do what you want to do.
- Say yes to something new, an invitation, an opportunity.
- Call an old friend and catch up on your lives.
- Spend time in silence.
- Walk barefoot in the grass, or play in the waves on the beach, or watch the clouds drift by in the sky.
- Write a love letter to yourself.
- Write a thank-you note to yourself.
- Take a walk in the moonlight.
- Make a delicious meal for yourself and serve it on your best china.

If there is to be Peace in the world,
There must be Peace in the nations.

If there is to be Peace in the nations,
There must be Peace in the cities.

If there is to be Peace in the cities,
There must be Peace between neighbors.

If there is to be Peace between neighbors,
There must be Peace in the home.

If there is to be Peace in the home,
There must be Peace in the Heart.

—Lao Tzu

Wisdom Affirmations for Reconnection and Coming Full Circle

- I am connected to everyone and everything at all times.
- The Universe orchestrates to bring us together, at various times, for various purposes.
- We are here to help each other learn and grow. I help others, and I am grateful for how others help me.
- I am still, and always, whole, complete, and perfect. My experiences have made me wiser, and clearer, and more grateful.

Afterword

An underlying urge to self-transformation possibly lies at the basis of all existence, finding expression in the process of growth, development, renewal, directed change, perfection.

—Lewis Mumford

Finding Closure
by Lissa Coffey

You and me were meant to be,

Maybe not for always—but for those moments in time.

We met as if by magic.

Drawn to each other,

Bringing something to this life that

For a while filled our needs in a way nothing else and no one else could.

We've seen our seasons,

We've made our choices.

We've learned and loved and grown through every experience.

And now the "we" that was, is back to me.

I recognize our relationship has changed.

I accept this change and all that comes with it.

I understand the reasons for it, and what will follow.

I integrate this change into my life to become more of myself.

I am grateful for the memories, the lessons learned, the moments shared.

There is peace in my mind and my heart.

I am whole, and complete, delighting in my natural state of being.

And so it is.

Acknowledgments

Thank you to all the people in my life who have experienced changes with me that enabled us to learn and grow. I may not have known it or understood it at the time, but your presence was a gift to me, and I totally love and appreciate you for it.

Thank you, Barbara Deal, for your insight, your steadfastness, your authenticity. I am a better writer because of you.

Thank you, Deepak Chopra, for your guidance and your shining example.

And a very special thank you to my online community of friends and subscribers. I love this journey that we are on together!

About the Author

Lissa Coffey is a lifestyle and relationship expert and frequent contributor to many national television shows, including *The Today Show*. She covers a variety of topics dealing with relationships, family, pop culture, lifestyle, and even sex. Lissa has been featured in *Redbook*, *Woman's Day*, and several other publications. She has traveled the country to local stations, both live and via satellite, as a spokesperson for various sponsored television tours.

Lissa is the author of four additional books and several e-books. Her most recent book is the best-selling *What's Your Dosha, Baby? Discover the Vedic Way for Compatibility in Life and Love.*

Lissa writes three different e-mail newsletters and has more than one hundred thousand subscribers around the world. She has several Web sites, including coffeytalk.com and whatsyourdosha.com. *CoffeyTalk: Ancient Wisdom, Modern Style,* is an Internet television show seen on YouTube, iTunes, and several other Internet channels. Lissa blogs on The Huffington Post and Intent.com, as well as on her own Web site.

As a television host and producer, Lissa was awarded a commendation from Los Angeles Mayor Antonio Villaraigosa for her work promoting health and wellness in her *Dosha Yoga* DVD.

Please visit Lissa's Web site (http://www.coffeytalk.com) for more information.

Resources

Lissa's free e-mail newsletters and online advice column:
www.coffeytalk.com

Learn about meditation:
www.psmeditation.com

"Heal Yourself with Ayurveda," Lissa's eight-week e-course with Daily Om:
www.dailyom.com

American Foundation for Suicide Prevention:
www.afsp.org

The Better Sleep Council (tips for getting a good night's sleep):
www.bettersleep.org

Children and Adults with Attention Deficit Disorder:
www.chadd.org

The Fred Society:
www.fredsociety.com

The Jenna Druck Foundation:
www.jennadruck.org

The Just Like My Child Foundation:
www.justlikemychild.org

Social Networking sites:
www.cafemom.com (for moms)
www.goodreads.com (for people who like to read)
www.intent.com (for people interested in bettering
the world)
www.soldiersangels.org (for mothers of soldiers)
www.widowsbond.com (for widows)
www.facebook.com (join Lissa's CoffeyTalk group)
www.twitter.com (follow Lissa @coffeytalk)

Information and ideas for name changes:
www.name-counsel.us

Hypnotherapy:
www.dicksutphen.com

Quizzes to get to know yourself better:
www.coffeytalk.com
www.whatsyourdosha.com
www.youniverse.com

Recommended Reading

Beattie, Melodie. *Codependent No More: How to Stop Controlling Others and Start Caring for Yourself.* Center City, MN: Publisher Name, 1992.

Carnegie, Dale. *How to Win Friends and Influence People.* New York: Pocket Books, 1936.

Chopra, Deepak. *The Path to Love: Spiritual Strategies for Healing.* New York: Three Rivers Press, 1997.

Coffey, Lissa. *What's Your Dosha, Baby? Discover the Vedic Way for Compatibility in Life and Love.* New York: Marlowe & Co., 2004.

Cohen, Alan. *Happily Even After: Can You Be Friends After Lovers?* Carlsbad, CA: Hay House Publishing, 1999.

Emmons, Robert. *Thanks: How the New Science of Gratitude Can Make You Happier.* New York: Houghton Mifflin, 2007.

Ford, Arielle. *The Soulmate Secret: Manifest the Love of Your Life Using the Law of Attraction.* New York: HarperOne, 2008.

Ford, Debbie. *Spiritual Divorce: Divorce as a Catalyst for an Extraordinary Life.* San Francisco: Harper San Francisco, 2001.

Foundation for Inner Peace. *A Course in Miracles.* Glen Allen, CA: Foundation for Inner Peace, 1976.

Hickland, Catherine. *The 30-Day Heartbreak Cure: Getting Over Him and Back Out There One Month from Today.* New York: Simon Spotlight Entertainment, 2009.

Kubler-Ross, Elisabeth, and David Kessler. *On Grief and Grieving: Finding the Meaning of Grief Through the Five Stages of Loss.* Location: Scribner, 2007.

Orloff, Judith. *Positive Energy: 10 Extraordinary Prescriptions for Transforming Fatigue, Stress & Fear into Vibrance, Strength & Love.* New York: Three Rivers Press, 2004.

Pert, Candace. *Molecules of Emotion: The Science Behind Mind-Body Medicine.* New York: Simon & Schuster, 1999.

Sutphen, Dick, and Tara Sutphen. *Soul Agreements.* Charlottesville, VA: Hampton Roads Publishing, 2005.

Tessina, Tina B. *It Ends With You: Grow Up and Out of Dysfunction.* Franklin Lakes, NJ: New Page Books, 2003.

Tipping, Colin C. *Radical Forgiveness: Making Room for the Miracle.* Location: Quest Publishing and Distribution, 2002.

Tripuri, B. V. *Aesthetic Vedanta: The Sacred Path of Passionate Love.* Eugene, OR: Mandala Publishing Group, 1998.

Vrajaprana, Pravrajika. *Vedanta: A Simple Introduction.* Hollywood, CA: Vedanta Press, 1999.

Ware, Ciji. *Rightsizing Your Life: Simplifying Your Surroundings While Keeping What Matters Most.* New York: Springboard Press, 2007.

Williamson, Marianne. *Enchanted Love: The Mystical Power of Intimate Relationships.* New York: Touchstone, 1999.

Williamson, Marianne. *The Age of Miracles: Embracing the New Midlife.* Carlsbad, CA: Hay House USA, 2008.

Made in the USA
Charleston, SC
28 January 2010